THE JET PROVOST

Martyn Chorlton

AMBERLEY

First published 2019

Amberley Publishing
The Hill, Stroud, Gloucestershire, GL5 4EP
www.amberley-books.com

Copyright © Martyn Chorlton, 2019

ISBN 978 1 4456 8117 7 (print)
ISBN 978 1 4456 8118 4 (ebook)

British Library Cataloguing in Publication Data.
A catalogue record for this book is available from the
British Library.

Origination by Amberley Publishing.
Printed in Great Britain.

Contents

RAF Training

The initial stage of training a potential military pilot in the art of flying has changed little since the dawn of flight; the basic principles, from a control and airmanship point of view, have changed little; and while aircraft have become more complex as additional roles and duties have been added, the basic theory of controlling a flying machine has changed little – with one major exception, when jet power began to replace piston power from the 1940s onwards. The jet engines, especially early variants, while relatively powerful, lacked an instant response. A big, powerful, well-handled piston engine could get you out of a world of trouble in an instant with a well-timed push on the throttle, while an early jet engine would leave you in a potentially precarious position as it slowly spooled back up to full power, by which time the pilot would be left red-faced at best or dead at worst! Training during the Second World War saw most of the fledgling pilots transition from the de Havilland Tiger Moth, via the North American Harvard and on to type. Even the introduction of the twin-engine, jet-powered Gloster Meteor in 1944 saw the same route taken. It was not until the arrival of the trainer variant of the Meteor (the RAF's first dedicated jet trainer) over four years later that a pilot could actually receive in the cockpit instruction thanks to a tandem seating arrangement, although this particular machine was far from being a 'primary' jet trainer.

Post-war, the RAF flying training system had not changed much since before the war, with the Tiger Moth and Harvard still providing the mainstay. However, changes were afoot: de Havilland Canada was about to introduce its highly successful tandem-seated Chipmunk (which would replace the Tiger Moth in the elementary role), while the Luton-based Percival Aircraft Ltd presented its Prentice, followed by the more successful Provost side-by-side piston-powered trainer. From 1948 onwards, a Prentice/Harvard training system was introduced by the RAF, later superseded by the Provost/Vampire system, the latter of which also lacked a dedicated jet trainer until the arrival of the de Havilland Vampire T.11 in 1952. As the RAF began to evolve into a jet-powered air force, the need to streamline basic flying training became apparent and other than the *ab initio* (beginner) stage, there was little need for wasting time and money in training a future jet pilot to fly a piston-powered primary trainer. The next stage was for a manufacturer that was already producing trainers for the RAF to step up to plate to design and build the RAF's first primary jet trainer. Percival would be that company.

Above: The third prototype Percival Provost T.1, WG503, which carried out its maiden flight from Luton on 24 February 1950. (R. L. Ward Collection)

Below: The second prototype Provost T.1, WE530, resting at Luton. Note the future Jet Provost lines. (R. L. Ward Collection)

All-British Company

Formed as the Percival Aircraft Company by Edgar Percival in 1933 at Gravesend, the company cut its teeth producing some very attractive light aircraft designs including the Gull, Vega Gull, Mew Gull and the larger Q.6 and Petrel twin-engined machines. By 1936, the growing company relocated to Luton and became Percival Aircraft Ltd. Not long after, the company produced its first military training aircraft in the shape of the P.28 Proctor, which first flew in October 1939. The Proctor served as a radio trainer and/or communications aircraft with the RAF and FAA until 1955 and the 1,143 that were built by Percival kept the company occupied for the bulk of the Second World War. Edgar Percival resigned from the company board during the Second World War so that he could serve with the RAFVR and, as a result, sold his remaining shares in the company, which became part of the long-established Hunting Group in 1944. The next design produced at Luton was the all-metal P.40 Prentice basic trainer. Designed to a 1943 Air Ministry Specification, the prototype first flew on 31 March 1946 and initially suffered a number of idiosyncrasies which were ironed out before more than 370 were delivered to the RAF. Prentice production was sub-contracted to Blackburn at Brough while Proctor and P.48 Merganser, P.50 Prince, P.54 Survey Prince, P.66 Pembroke and President production continued at Luton.

In the meantime, the Hunting design team, led by Polish-born Henry Millicer, was beavering away at a replacement for the mediocre Prentice, producing the excellent P.56 Provost. The Alvis Leonides-powered Provost was an attractive low-wing monoplane with a fixed undercarriage and a side-by-side cockpit. The 500 hp Leonides pushed the little Provost to a maximum speed of 200 mph and was one of more than thirty design proposals produced to Air Ministry Specification T.16/48 (OR.257), which called specifically for a Prentice replacement. The prototype, powered by an Armstrong Siddeley Cheetah engine, first flew on 24 February 1950 and, following evaluation against the only other design to leave the drawing board, the Handley Page H.P.R.2, the Provost won an initial order contract for 200 aircraft on 29 May 1951. The total RAF order reached 388 aircraft and the popular P.56 Provost served the RAF from 1953 until 1969, although the type had long since been replaced in the primary training role by the time the last examples were withdrawn from service.

As a company, Percival followed one of two roads laid out for it that all British aircraft manufacturers were destined to take. In 1954, the company became Hunting Percival Aircraft Ltd, and three years later Hunting Aircraft Ltd, but the big change came in 1960 when the manufacturer was absorbed into BAC, along with Bristol, English Electric and Vickers-Armstrong.

Luton Airport.

Percival Aircraft Ltd moved from Gravesend to Luton in 1936 and remained there, albeit under the BAC umbrella, until 1965. (R. L. Ward Collection)

Enter the P.84

Percival recognised the need for an *ab initio* jet-powered trainer at a very early stage and set about designing a new aircraft which relied heavily on major components from the piston-powered Provost, following an award to Percival of an Air Ministry contract on 8 June 1953. The new aircraft began to take shape under the company designation P.84, the initial design proposals being drawn up by Leslie George Frise FRAeS (1895–1979), the Technical Director and Chief Engineer, who took over the role from Arthur Bage in 1948. Frise had a great deal of experience in the aircraft industry, having served the Bristol Aeroplane Company for thirty-two years before joining Percival. Behind him were great designs such as the Beaufighter, Beaufort, Blenheim, Brabazon and the well-known Frise slotted aileron to name a few. With Percival, he would go on to design the naval variants of the Prince and Sea Prince and the piston Provost.

In using the piston Provost as the foundation for the P.84, the biggest challenge was positioning the jet engine. The chosen unit was the 1,640 lb static thrust Armstrong Siddeley Viper 101 (ASV.5), similar to the engine that powered the GAF Jindivik target drone, although unlike the radio-controlled machine, the P.84's was not expendable! Because of the very nature of the target drone's work, the Jindivik's powerplant only had a life of ten hours but provided the basis for a very light unit that could give a jet trainer the endurance it needed to take part in a training syllabus. Frise's early ideas for the P.84 saw the Viper engine positioned in the nose, presumably with the cockpit set well back and the jet pipe exiting below the aircraft. This was a logical first thought as virtually all piston power plants were installed in the front of the aircraft, with the odd exception. However, further thought resulted in the Viper being placed in the middle of fuselage, directly above the wing, with twin air intakes in front of the leading edge and a tail pipe which extended through the rear fuselage, exiting below the tail plane.

The prototype P.84 Jet Provost quickly took shape thanks to utilising the main Provost structure. The forward fuselage was the most modified part of the aircraft, although use was still made of the Provost canopy. Another major difference was that the Jet Provost would have a retractable tricycle undercarriage and, to accommodate the nose wheel, a pair of beams were installed in the lower forward fuselage. The prototype's main undercarriage units were the same as the Provost's, giving the aircraft quite a high ground clearance, which was necessary for the piston-powered tail dragger. A 3-foot extension, strengthening and a slight re-contour of the rear fuselage below the fin was needed to accommodate the long internal jet pipe. A dorsal fin was installed to compensate for the bigger side area which was created by the redesigned cockpit and a long ventral tail bumper was fitted to protect the fuselage should the aircraft over-rotate on take-off. The layout of the cockpit had the same side-by-side arrangement of the original Provost, but with revised instrumentation.

Above: A model mock-up of the prototype Jet Provost T.1, XD674, exposing the Viper engine, tail-pipe and structure. (Percival Aircraft Ltd (PY3625) via Martin Richmond Photos)

Right: Hunting Percival Aircraft Ltd advert circa 1956 promoting the Jet Provost in T.1 (airborne) and T.2 versions (main advert). (Hunting Group via R. L. Ward Collection)

The Jet Provost T.1

The Secretary of State for Air, George Ward, announced in the Commons on 12 March 1953 that Percival Aircraft had been awarded a contract to manufacture ten Jet Provost T.1s. These aircraft, serialled XD674 to XD680 and XD692 to XD694, would be used for service evaluation and were ordered under Contract 6/Aircraft/9265/CB.5(a). The latter contract also included an eleventh aircraft, later given the civilian registration of G-ABOU, which would serve as company demonstrator.

The prototype Hunting Percival Jet Provost T.1, XD674, made its maiden flight from Luton in the hands of company Chief Test Pilot Richard 'Dick' G. Wheldon on 26 June 1954. Wheldon joined the RAF in 1936, serving with Bomber Command and Maintenance Command before joining Percival Aircraft in 1947. Wheldon was heavily involved in the development of test flying of the Merganser, Prentice and Prince, and also carried out the maiden flight of the piston Provost. He was well known at the then annual SBAC display at Farnborough and, before retiring from Hunting Percival in 1957, he had performed in ten consecutive shows. It was in September 1954 that the Jet Provost T.1 made its public debut at Farnborough.

Post-Farnborough, a number of modifications were made to XD674 which included the removal of the dorsal fin and this was compensated for by an extended ventral fin. To improve the low-speed handling qualities of the aircraft, fillets were installed at the leading

The prototype Jet Provost T.1, XD674, about to be rolled out for the first time at Luton in June 1954. *(Percival Aircraft Ltd (PY4044) via Martin Richmond Photos)*

wing roots. XD674 arrived at the A&AEE, Boscombe Down, on 5 November 1954 for trial work and would return to Wiltshire again in 1956 for blower tunnel trials. XD674 was destined never to enter RAF service but instead was loaned to Armstrong Siddeley Motors on two occasions, once in May 1955 and again in April 1956. Operating out of Bitteswell, the aircraft was involved in further development work of the Viper ASV.5 and the more powerful ASV.8. XD674's flying career came to an end in 1958 when it was allocated the instructional airframe number 7570M and dispatched to No. 71 MU at Bicester. The aircraft was moved to Finningley in 1965, Swinderby in 1977 and moved on to St Athan in 1979 before arriving at its current home, the RAF Museum, RAF Cosford, in November 1985.

Above: Jet Provost T.1 XD674 during an early flight, or possibly its maiden flight, from Luton in the hands of company Chief Test Pilot Richard 'Dick' G. Wheldon on 26 June 1954; note lack of roundels. (Hunting Group via R. L. Ward Collection)

Right: XD674 captured at the A&AEE, Boscombe Down, during trials in late 1954. (*The Aeroplane* via Martin Richmond Photos)

XD674 was not destined to enter RAF service but was involved in a great deal of trial work with the manufacturers, the A&AEE and Armstrong Siddeley. (*The Aeroplane* via Martin Richmond Photos)

Retired to the care of No. 71 MU at RAF Bicester, XD674 was allocated the maintenance number 7570M. The aircraft is pictured at RAF Gaydon on 16 September 1967. (R. L. Ward)

Evaluation and Service Trials

Of the ten Jet Provost T.1s built, nine of them were destined to enter RAF service and carry out a two-phase service trial. Phase 'A' began on 22 June 1955 when two T.1s, XD676 and XD679, were delivered to the Central Flying School (CFS) at RAF South Cerney in Gloucestershire. Eventually, seven T.1s would join the CFS, with XD677 arriving in August 1955 following a landing accident involving XD679. Experienced basic and advanced flying instructors (AFIs) put the T.1s through an intensive flying programme for a period of 111 flying hours. During this period, the general handling of the aircraft was fully explored, as were the general operating qualities, which were found to be excellent on both counts. On top of this, instructors, operating in pairs, quickly formulated a basic training syllabus, during which time ten flying instructors were fully converted on to type. By the end of the flying programme, the Jet Provost was highly recommended by the CFS to serve as an *ab initio* jet trainer. Recommending a course length of twenty-three weeks, which included 160 hours of flying training, it was time for the Jet Provost to be evaluated with the students at the controls.

The unit chosen to carry out the RAF's first 'jet' course was No. 2 FTS, operating from RAF Hullavington, a unit which had been only operating the piston-powered Provost T.1 and a few Chipmunks since 1954. So, as part of 'Phase 'B' of the official Service Trials and under the unofficial code name 'White Mouse' (as in the blind leading the blind), the first Jet Provost T.1s arrived at Wiltshire in August 1955. No. 113 (Jet) Course began on 2 September 1955 and comprised eighteen students, none of whom were streamed specifically for this historic course. The course progressed with few dramas and, on average, the students with previous flying experience reached the first solo stage in 9 hours 50 minutes, and 11 hours 15 minutes for those without. Seven students were selected during the course to carry out advanced training on the Vampire at No. 8 FTS, RAF Swinderby, to see if they had progressed further than a student following the piston route. Each student, on average, flew four to five hours on the Vampire during March and April 1956 before returning to Hullavington.

The first course ended in July 1956 and the second, No. 120 (Jet) Course, began immediately after. Sixteen students were assigned to the course and one of them, Acting Pilot Officer Tony Haig-Thomas, has vivid memories of the experience:

In the early 1950s, when most front line aircraft were jet powered, it seemed anomalous to train pilots in the totally different field of big piston technology with superchargers, constant speed units, automatic boost control, cowling gills to cool the cylinder heads, radiator shutters, oil coolers, inter coolers, fuel in gallons and endurance in hours when they would be operational with Jet Pipe Temperatures, percentage RPM, and endurance in minutes. We were to fly the Jet Provost T.1, to see if pilots could learn to fly jet aircraft from the beginning: the trials were coded 'White Mouse'. There were three courses and ours was the second. Being a jet, the aircraft was of course much easier to fly than the piston-engined Provost but, whereas the piston pilots needed handling skills, the Jetties had to cope with oxygen, retractable undercarriage, airbrakes and very little fuel. We had to climb through cloud, make cross country flights, and descend through cloud, solo, returning with no fuel for a diversion. Retrospectively I am amazed – and still cannot believe – how easily it was accomplished by all the students on No. 120 (Jet) Course. I liked the 'Jet' bit!

Our Course settled in and after a fortnight's ground school we were split into two flights, half to fly in the mornings, the other half in the afternoons with the afternoon teams getting the morning slot the next day. Sixteen of us started but only eleven finished with the other five being 'washed out' at various times over the nine months. Reasons varied from failing to go solo, air sickness, lack of ability or, later on, from lack of ability to fly on instruments – a very important jet requirement ... my life's dream was about to start. It was 19 July, 1956.

I had not realised how many cockpit drills had to be performed for each flight – it had just not crossed my mind. There were external checks, pre-start checks, after start checks, pre-take off checks, checks during take-off, after take-off checks, fuel checks (all the time), pre-aerobatic checks, returning to base checks, downwind checks, finals checks and shut down checks.

I loved the flying but practically reduced my poor instructor to tears over all these checks, or rather my lack of ability to remember them; fifty years later as a Jet Provost instructor myself (unpaid) I realise that we needed a simulator or cockpit drill trainer. It was very difficult to find an empty cockpit to practice drills, as the aircraft were either flying, being turned round between flights or worked on in the hangars. Whichever it was the last thing that was needed was 16 students each trying to find an empty cockpit to practise all the endless checks.

Tony carried out his last flight at No. 2 FTS with his regular instructor, Flt Sgt A. 'Jock' Naismith, on 22 February 1957 before being posted to No. 8 FTS in April 1957. There had been very few incidents during Tony's course, although 'Jock' Naismith was involved in the most serious on 20 August 1956. Jock's student that day was Plt Off E. P. Kendall in Jet Provost T.1 XD692. During a routine training sortie a wing over was performed at 10,000 ft, following which the pilot then throttled back in preparation for a practice forced landing. However, the Viper engine flamed out and could not be restarted before descending through cloud, which was broken through at just 800 ft. A small cornfield was quickly selected, 8 miles west-north-west of Hullavington, for a landing but on touchdown the aircraft slid across the field and struck a wall on the far side. Neither Naismith nor Kendall were injured but the RAF had lost its first Jet Provost; the aircraft was deemed beyond repair and was later scrapped at Hullavington later in the year.

The last of three evaluation courses came to an end in November 1957 and all of those involved, from senior staff and instructors to students, were full of praise for the little jet trainer. The CFS Examining Wing was particularly complimentary, stating:

> The student standard reflects most favourably on the aircraft's suitability as an ab initio trainer; compared to the average pupil, the jet-trained student has, in a shorter time in the air, achieved a more dextrous and better mental approach to the art of modern flying. His repertoire of aerobatic manoeuvres for example, is more extensive and flown with much more spirit and accuracy...

The manufacturers were understandably very happy with the CFS report and endorsed it with their own round-up of the 18-month long evaluation period:

> 50 RAF pupils have now been introduced to the Jet Provost in the last two years. Of these, 35 had no previous flying experience; 15 had flown light piston-engine types. The nine aircraft at RAF Hullavington flew 4,000 hours and made 11,000 landings. Engine reliability showed an increase between service from 100 hours to 300 hours and a saving of £3,000 on flying alone the Jet Provost has proved itself as the only jet trainer capable of such economical training.

Both the RAF and Hunting Percival were supported by the Secretary of State for Air, who announced on 8 February 1957 that the Jet Provost was the perfect aircraft for providing all-through jet training and a large production order would be placed.

In the meantime, the remaining seven available Jet Provost T.1s were transferred to the CFS for jet conversion training and for the final phase of the students' courses. However, the opportunity was not lost to 'fly the flag' and show off the RAF's new jet trainer and the main reason as to why the T.1s were delivered to the CFS was to form an aerobatic team. Led by Flt Lt Norman Giffin, the 'CFS Jet Aerobatic Team' of four aircraft was flown by volunteer instructors. Repainted in an attractive red and white colour scheme, the team made its debut at the SBAC, Farnborough, in September 1958. The T.1s were destined to remain with the CFS until November 1959, when a more advanced mark of the Jet Provost took over the helm.

Above: The young student pilots' faces are as fresh as the aircraft they are training with. Jet Provost T.1s of No. 2 FTS, RAF Hullavington, provide the backdrop. (Air Ministry (PRB11430) via Martin Richmond Photos)

Below: Instructor and student prepare for a sortie in a No. 2 FTS Jet Provost T.1 at Hullavington. Note the long ladder on the port side of the aircraft – a feature that was dispensed with in later variants. (Air Ministry (*PRB11434*) via Martin Richmond Photos)

Above: Jet Provost T.1 XD693 tucks up its long undercarriage to begin another sortie with No. 2 FTS. Note the piston Provost T.1 in the background. (Air Ministry (PRB11418) via Martin Richmond Photos)

Below: No. 2 FTS Provost T.1s on the line at Hullavington; the aircraft are XD675, XD676, XD677, XD678 and XD693, all of which were destined to be transferred to the CFS after the 'Hullavington Experiment' was finished. (*The Aeroplane* (17688) via Martin Richmond Photos)

Above: A flight lieutenant flying instructor delivers a final briefing before a sortie for a couple of No. 2 FTS student pilots. XD693 provides the backdrop. (Air Ministry (PRB11429) via Martin Richmond Photos)

Below: The RAF wanted the world to see its new jet trainer just as much as Hunting wanted to sell it to the world; the former were more successful than the latter. (*The Aeroplane* (17688) via Martin Richmond Photos)

Above: Two CFS Jet Provost T.1s, XD678 and XD679, of the 'CFS Jet Aerobatic Team' get airborne at Farnborough in 1958. (Shell Aviation via R. L. Ward Collection)

Below: Images of CFS Jet Provost T.1s are rare because of the short time period they served the unit. XD679 is captured in 1959 only months before the aircraft was withdrawn from service. (R. L. Ward Collection)

The CFS Jet Aerobatic Team, led by Flt Lt Norman Giffin, performs for the camera prior to the 1958 SBAC at Farnborough. (*The Aeroplane* (18773) via Martin Richmond Photos)

Take Two – The Core Aircraft

It was now clear that a jet-powered basic trainer was both feasible and a workable idea, the company set about designing the aircraft into a more practical proposition. Work had already begun on the Jet Provost T.2 (still retaining the designation P.84) before the Secretary of State for Air's commitment as a private venture and one of these aircraft, the tenth production T.1, XD894, was actually trialled by No. 2 FTS during the T.1 evaluation period as the prototype T.2. Only four T.2s were destined to be built as pre-production aircraft.

The T.2 incorporated a number of changes, the most obvious of which was the undercarriage. The long-legged T.1 had a tendency to 'walk' across rough ground and was one of the many features of the original aircraft that were installed for economic reasons. A new, shorter and stronger undercarriage was installed; it was so much shorter in fact that the crew could actually board the aircraft via a sprung foot pad in each intake fairing and a walkway along the wing root, rather than needing a specialist ladder. The undercarriage's original and reliable pneumatic system was also replaced by a more powerful hydraulic system.

The fuselage of the Jet Provost T.2 comprised two sections. The forward section extended from the nose of the aircraft through to the rear of the engine bay. At this point, the forward section ended at a bulkhead, which was attached to the rear spar of the wing. Seven sub-assemblies made up the forward section, comprising a bottom assembly, a pair of side assemblies, a canopy, decking, access panels for the engine and a hinged nose cap.

Construction of the bottom assembly included a pair of longitudinal beams which were designed to soak up the impact loads from the nose wheel. These beams also formed a compartment into which the nose wheel retracted. Further rearwards, a pair of transverse beams were located, one to provide attachment fittings for the main spar and the second for the trailing, subsidiary spar. The two transverse beams also provided support for the floor of the engine bay and the cockpit. The bottom assembly was finished with a metal skin which was supported by frames and 'Z' section stringers, complete with access panels so that entry could be gained to the equipment that was located under the floors.

To the bottom assembly were attached the two side assemblies which again were constructed of frames and 'Z' section stringers, bolstered by channel section, light alloy longerons. The side assemblies were joined by a decking that held the cockpit windscreen, which was made up of five panels, all of which were optically flat. Solid bulkheads were installed in front of and behind the cockpit, topped off by a single-piece manually operated sliding canopy. The spacious, now accessible nose compartment, thanks to a hinged cap, now contained radio and electrical equipment, an oxygen charging point and the aircraft's batteries.

The rear section of the fuselage was recontoured to better accommodate the long jet pipe. Constructed in four sections – a pair of sides, the top and bottom – the structure was semi-monocoque and was made up of frames and 'Z' section stringers skinned in light alloy.

The wings comprised a single main spar and a subsidiary spar – the latter of which was designed to disperse the loads that were applied by the ailerons, slotted flaps and spoilers. Internally, the ribs and formers are full depth in front of the main spar and the chord of the wing was extended with a fairing. The latter, in its training aircraft guise, would house a pair of taxiing lamps in its leading edge, although plans were already afoot for this to be made ready for a pair of machine guns or cannon for future armed variants. Both ribs and formers continued aft between the main and subsidiary spars with an auxiliary spar, firstly designed to distribute forces from the main undercarriage unit and secondly to create a compartment for the unit to retract into.

Each wing also had lined compartments which were designed to hold three bag-type/ flexible fuel tanks with a 165-gallon total capacity. Two of these compartments were housed in the leading edge of the wing while the third was located to the rear of the main spar, outboard of the undercarriage. The fin, rudder, tailplane and elevators were virtually identical to the original piston Provost with the exception of a few refinements.

The undercarriage of the Jet Provost T.2 was a much tidier arrangement; the main wheel units retracted inwards and the nose wheel forwards. The main wheels were fitted with hydraulically operated disc brakes. A single hydraulic ram positioned under the cockpit floor powered all of the undercarriage units and wheel bay doors. The nose wheel doors were operated by push-rods and bell-crank levers, while the main doors were controlled by push-rods and levers connected to sprockets that were driven by retraction chains. Should a failure occur, the undercarriage could be lowered by injecting compressed air on the 'down' side of the hydraulic ram and a small device, mounted on the top of the nose wheel leg, made sure that the unit was centred before it was retracted.

Power for the T.2 was provided by a single-shaft Armstrong Siddeley Viper (ASV.8) turbojet which developed 1,750 lbs of thrust at 13,800 rpm. The Viper had a seven-stage axial compressor, an annular combustion chamber and a single-stage turbine. On each side of the engine was a tripod mounting which was bolted to the wing attachment beams, backed up by a tie-strut at the rear of the turbojet to stop the powerplant pitching. The bulkhead at the front of the engine hosted an accessory gearbox which gained its power via a shaft from the engine.

The prototype T.2, XD694, carried out its maiden flight, once again in the hands of 'Dick' Wheldon, from Luton on 1 September 1955. By December, XD694 had logged 143 flying hours during manufacturer's test flying before it was sent to the A&AEE at RAF Boscombe Down for service acceptance trials. XD694 entered RAF service when it was transferred to No. 2 FTS at Hullavington for comparative trials with the T.1. The few students (possibly only four) who were lucky enough to fly this rare aircraft converted easily to the new Jet Provost, the main variation being the difference between the long-legged T.1 and the shorter-legged T.2; the 100 lbs extra thrust from the ASV.8 was barely noticeable.

XD694, with 260 flying hours under its belt, was transferred to Armstrong Siddeley, operating from Bitteswell and Filton from June 1957, taking part in continuing engine development. With the latter completed, the aircraft was surplus to requirements and was flown to No. 27 MU at RAF Shawbury, from where it was sold for scrap in October 1960.

The second of four T.2s that were destined to be built was G-AOHD, which made its maiden flight in March 1956. The aircraft was first seen in public at the British Lockheed International Aerobatic Competition in July 1956, and with 'Dick' Wheldon at the controls, was placed fourth in the event. By early 1957, G-AOHD became a company demonstration aircraft, specifically aimed at potential sales in very cold and very hot and high environments. In April 1958, 'Dick' Wheldon took the aircraft to Sweden and then to Finland in March. By April, the aircraft was being dismantled and shipped out to Trinidad before embarking on a busy tour of South America. Flown by company test pilot 'Dicky' Rumbelow, G-AOHD progressed through Venezuela, Colombia, Chile, Peru, Argentina, Uruguay and then Brazil in late July. The aircraft then returned to Luton in another crate on 12 August. While the company was not awash with orders for the Jet Provost (only Venezuela would place an order) the tour was classed as a huge success and the aircraft performed impeccably. The tour had covered 8,400 miles, logged 178 flying hours and had been operated from twenty-seven airfields.

G-AOHD was dispatched to Australia in March 1959 for a six-month trial with the RAAF. The aircraft was given the RAAF serial A99-001 and was flown by No. 1 BFTS at Point Cook. Just two students were selected from No. 35 Pilot Training Course to fly the Jet Provost in a comparative trial, while the remainder of the course continued flying the CAC CA-25 Winjeel (an aircraft heavily influenced by the piston Provost). Just like in the RAF at the time, the students then progressed on to the Vampire, which was the scenario the RAAF chose to keep until the arrival of the Macchi MB-326 in 1967. The Jet Provost was destined to remain in Australia and, because of this, it is the only T.2 survivor and is currently in permanent storage at the RAAF Museum at Point Cook.

The third T.2 pre-production aircraft was originally supposed to have the civilian registration G-APVY but this was never taken up because this aircraft would take a different path. Allocated the 'B' class test serial G-23-1 (the 'G-23' part was unique to Percival/Hunting), the aircraft was modified into the prototype T.3 instead.

The fourth and final pre-production T.2 was registered as G-AOUS and first flew in August 1956. The first task for this Jet Provost was to take part in a demonstration tour of Canada and the USA. The RCAF had already sent a number of representatives to Luton in 1955 to assess the Jet Provost and it was one of a number of jet training aircraft which had been selected for further evaluation in Canada to replace the ageing Harvard fleet; the others included the Fouga CM-170 Magister and the Canadair CT-114 Tutor. G-AOUS generated a great deal of interest during the tour; in Canada, a number of service pilots flew the aircraft from RCAF Ottawa and Trenton. Like their USAF colleagues, all were full of praise for the little trainer but undoubtedly the home-grown Tutor was always the favourite for the RCAF and, unsurprisingly, was selected as the primary jet trainer.

Once back in the UK, G-AOUS served with the RAE before its engine was replaced with a 2,500 lb static thrust Viper (ASV.11) in August 1958. The aircraft was then unofficially redesignated as the T.2B. This significant increase in power made the T.2B a good performer and, on 13 July 1959, the aircraft was entered into the London to Paris Air Race, sponsored by the *Daily Mail*.

It was back on the sales road for G-AOUS again in October 1959; this time to Portugal to compete against the Cessna T-37A Tweet. Given the temporary Portuguese Air Force serial '5803', a wheels-up landing on 30 October may not have done the Jet Provost's cause much good and the T-37 was eventually chosen. The type remained in PAF service until 1992.

Unfortunately, tragedy struck on 16 November 1960 during a routine test flight over Bedfordshire. With company test pilot Lt-Cdr J. R. S. 'Jack' Overbury RN at the controls, the aircraft was being recovered from a dive at the maximum design speed when positive 'G' forced the nose wheel undercarriage to lower. The entire leg and the undercarriage bay doors were ripped off under the stress and the sudden nose-up, violent pitch change overstressed the aircraft, causing the wings to detach and the rest of the aircraft to disintegrate. Overbury stood no chance and was killed, while the remains of G-AOUS crashed at Langford Common, 3 miles south of Biggleswade.

The last production Jet Provost T.1, XD694, became the prototype T.2, and was first flown in this configuration on 1 September 1955. (R. L. Ward Collection)

The most obvious difference between the T.1 and T.2 was the replacement of the former's long-legged undercarriage – a remnant of the piston Provost. (R. L. Ward Collection)

Built as a private venture, G-AOHD was the first of three 'pure' Jet Provost T.2s and was destined to be the only example of the breed to survive today. (C. P. Smith via David Westwood)

Above: Ex-G-AOHD, serialled A99-001, during its brief evaluation with the RAAF. The aircraft remained in Australia and is preserved at the RAAF Museum, Point Cook. (R. Holland, via R. L. Ward Collection)

Below: A very rare image of T.2 G-23-1 before it became the T.3 prototype, in company with the final T.2 to be built, G-AOUS. (Hunting Group via R. L. Ward Collection)

Above: G-AOUS, following conversion as the Bristol Siddeley testbed for the Viper 11, designated T.2B, on finals into Farnborough on 12 September 1959. (R. L. Ward)

Below: T.2B G-AOUS with the temporary Portuguese Air Force serial '5803' during its competition with the Cessna T-37A in October 1959. (R. L. Ward Collection)

The Production Machine – The T.3

As mentioned earlier, the pre-production T.2, G-23-1, was selected as the prototype for the full production T.3 variant. Learning a great deal from the T.1 and T.2 variants, not to mention feedback from the students, instructors and test pilots at the A&AEE, conversion work began on the aircraft at Luton in early 1958. Modifications included a rearranged cockpit complete with a blind-flying instrument panel. The windscreen was replaced with a single-piece clear vision version and a Mk.2 sliding cockpit canopy further improved visibility and accessibility. Standard production wings were installed, complete with tip tanks, and power was provided by a Viper 103 (ASV.9) turbojet.

By April 1958, the aircraft was in the hands of the A&AEE for handling and performance trials. While the reports back from the test pilots were generally favourable, in that the aircraft was easy to fly, the aircraft was described as too benign. It was, effectively, far too easy to fly and nowhere near as challenging as the piston Provost was. The worry was that students of just below par ability would progress further into their flying training, where a more challenging aircraft would expose their inabilities earlier. The lack of ejection seats in G-23-1 was the only other serious criticism by the A&AEE.

G-23-1, re-serialled XN117, went on to take part in the Venom Replacement Trial at Khormaksar, Aden, in mid-1958 in company with the Hawker Hunter and the lightweight fighter version of the Folland Gnat. Despite being armed with machine guns and pylons for rockets and bombs, the Jet Provost stood no chance of winning the competition, which would see the more capable Hunter being chosen for the role. The aircraft then left Aden for a tour of India and Pakistan, returning to Luton later in the year to be converted as the first T.51 for the Royal Ceylon Air Force.

Following the Secretary of State for Air's announcement in early 1957, a production order for 100 Jet Provost T.3s was placed under Contract 6/Aircraft/14157/CB.5(a) on 9 August 1957. The comments by the A&AEE were taken seriously and further modifications to the design included the installation of a pair of Martin Baker Mk.4P ejection seats. For the structure to cope with the latter, the rear bulkhead behind the cockpit was strengthened and sloped. Rebecca 8 with DF, UHF radio equipment, complete replacement of all pneumatic systems with hydraulic and a 1,750 lb static thrust Viper 102 (ASV.8) were now standard features of the T.3. As mentioned, the wings were little different from those fitted to the T.2, other than tip-tank lugs for a pair of 45-gallon non-jettisonable fuel tanks.

The first production Jet Provost T.3, XM346, carried out its maiden flight from Luton on 22 June 1958 and, along with the next six aircraft off the line, was dispatched to the A&AEE for various handling and service acceptance trials. It was more than a year before the first Jet Provost T.3 was officially handed over to the RAF in a low-key ceremony at Luton. Deliveries of the first production batch continued until July 1960, by which time a second order for a further 100 T.3s had been placed under Contract KC/E/031 – deliveries beginning in August 1960 and continuing until February 1962.

By the early 1970s, the T.3 and even later variants of the Jet Provost were in need of an upgrade, specifically in the radio and navigation equipment department. One T.3, XN629, was selected as the prototype aircraft for these new avionic systems, the work being carried out by BAC at Warton. Under Contract KA5(c)/466/CBA.5(c), eighty-six aircraft were converted to the new T.3A standard, the first aircraft, XM357, arriving at Warton for conversion in June 1973. The new equipment installed aboard the T.3A would ensure compliance with the latest air traffic control requirements and would certainly contribute to the type's longevity. Instrumentation included new VOR ILS, a civil DME, a Sperry CL6 compass, a VHF radio and a standby Ferranti Attitude Indicator. The modification period lasted until 9 August 1976, when the last T.3A to be upgraded was delivered to RAF Leeming.

Originally built as a Jet Provost T.2, this is the prototype T.3, G-23-1, after roll-out at Luton in May 1956. The cockpit windscreen and canopy are now a much tidier arrangement than the original T.1 and 2. (Hunting Group via R. L. Ward Collection)

The prototype Jet Provost T.3, serialled XN117, pictured before departing to RAF Khormaksar for the Venom Replacement Trial in mid-1958. (Hunting Group via R. L. Ward Collection)

Above: Early production Jet Provost T.3s on the grass at Luton prior to delivery to several trials units, including the A&AEE, in June 1958. (Hunting Group via R. L. Ward Collection)

Below: The first production Jet Provost T.3, XM346, being put through its paces. The aircraft saw service with the MoS, A&AEE, CFS, No. 6 FTS and the RAFC before ending its days at Thorney Island for fire practice in 1969. (Hunting Group via R. L. Ward Collection)

Above: The third production Jet Provost T.3 had a short flying career with the manufacturers and the A&AEE. The aircraft was lost with the latter on 4 September 1958, returning from Farnborough following a false fire warning. (Hunting Group via R. L. Ward Collection)

Right: No. 2 FTS shows off its brand-new Jet Provost T.3s in March 1960. (Central Press Photos Ltd via R. L. Ward Collection)

More Power – The T.4

The task of raising the performance of the Jet Provost had been on the agenda from the outset and the RAF was particularly keen to have a jet trainer which could spend more time at altitude for upper air work. The powerful 2,500 lb static thrust Viper 202 (ASV.11) had already been trialled in T.2 G-AOUS in 1958. The engine proved successful, generating 40 per cent more power, which was felt, and most appreciated, during take-off. In turn, the climb rate decreased significantly. Externally, the T.4 differed very little from the T.3, while internally new engine bearers were required for the Viper 202 and the dorsal air ducts were marginally increased in size.

A pair of Jet Provost T.3s, XN467 and XN468, were removed from production to serve as prototype T.4s. XN467 made its maiden flight on 15 July 1960 in the hands of company Chief Test Pilot Stan Oliver, the second prototype, XN468, taking to the air the following month. The latter aircraft made the T.4s public debut at the SBAC, Farnborough, in September in company with T.3 XN462.

Both XN467 and XN468 spent the remainder of 1960 and the bulk of 1962 being tested and trialled, but it was clear from the outset that this was the aircraft that the Air Ministry wanted. An initial production order for 100 T.4s was placed under Contract KC/E/041. Deliveries commenced to the RAF from October 1961 and continued until December 1962. Two early production T.4s, XP549 and XP550, joined the CFS at RAF Little Rissington on 23 November 1961. A second production order for fifty more T.4s was delivered between January and October 1963 under Contract KC/E/057 and a third and final batch for thirty-five more T.4s was delivered between October 1963 and September 1964 under Contract KC/E/070.

The second of two Jet Provost T.3s removed from the production line to serve as prototype T.4s was XN468. The aircraft went on to serve with No. 1 FTS, the RAFC and the CFS before being SOC in October 1971. (Hunting Group via R. L. Ward Collection)

A pristine example of a Jet Provost and the first production T.4, XP547. After trials with the A&AEE, XP547 had a long career with the RAFC, CATCS, MoD(PE), SRF and 1 TWU before retiring to RAF Cosford as an instructional airframe. (Hunting Group via R. L. Ward Collection)

Jet Provost T.4 XP547 in company with English Electric Lightning T.4 XM974. (Hunting Group via R. L. Ward Collection)

The very first Jet Provost T.4 to enter RAF was XP547, delivered to the CFS on 23 December 1961. (R. L. Ward Collection)

31

The Pressurised T.5

As implied with the introduction of the T.4, the need for training sorties to be performed above 20,000 ft during course training was vital. However, the downside to carrying out this work on a regular basis in an unpressurised aircraft was the same problem often suffered by deep sea divers – the 'bends'.

When Hunting proposed a Jet Provost with a pressurised cockpit to the Ministry of Aviation in 1961, the RAF did not actually have an official requirement for such a feature. Hunting stated that a modified T.4 would provide the airframe, although this idea was shelved because the fatigue of this variant was already predicted to be short due to its high-altitude work. With the latter in mind, it was decided that a new aircraft was needed and this was officially announced at the SBAC, Farnborough, in 1962 as the Hunting 145. A complex project, the preliminary design work was completed by late 1964, by which time the Ministry of Aviation had shown enough interest to issue a development contract. The project, which began as a private venture, had become the BAC 145.

Accommodating a fully pressurised cockpit resulted in the forward fuselage of the Jet Provost being completely redesigned forward of the rear spar. The aircraft, which would be designated as the Jet Provost T.5, was over a foot longer than the previous mark. The forward fuselage was not only longer but was also more aerodynamically efficient. The aircraft's batteries were relocated to the rear of the fuselage and the pressurisation and air conditioning system was mounted in their place. The canopy was also replaced with a rearward-sliding, high-visibility version which would later (1975/76) be equipped with a miniature detonation chord (MDC). However, only sixty-one examples would be modified with this feature.

The wings of the T.5 would be fitted with four hard points as per an armed export variant. Again, the RAF had no specific requirement for such a feature but, as the export wings had a longer fatigue life, they decided to choose them for the T.5, thus reducing redesign and manufacturing costs. The wing retained all the components that were needed to attach tip tanks, although these would not be needed for the T.5 as the internal wing capacity was a healthy 263.5 gallons. The fuel was contained within four interconnected tanks per wing, all of which were gravity-fed via a refuelling point on the upper surface. The T.4's 2,500 lb Viper 202 (ASV.11) was retained for the T.5.

Two aircraft, XS230 and XS231, the last two production T.4s, were chosen to serve as prototype T.5 (aka T.5P) aircraft in 1965. Both of these aircraft actually left the production line as T.4s, XS230 going into store with No. 27 MU at RAF Shawbury before being returned to Luton in 1965 for conversion. XS231 also briefly operated as a T.4, the aircraft being retained by BAC for development flying until its conversion began at Luton in 1965. There was some delay before the aircraft would be ready, initially due to the takeover of Hunting by BAC followed by the subsequent closure of Luton and then the move north to

Warton in Lancashire. It was not until August 1966 that both of the T.5 prototypes arrived at Warton. As a result, XS230 did not carry out its maiden flight until 28 February 1967 with Reg Stock at the controls and Jimmy Dell alongside. The flight only lasted 30 minutes and, although promising, several modifications would have to be made before the RAF was happy with the aircraft.

Work on the second prototype was more advanced and had taken a different route before becoming the second prototype T.5. XS231 was converted to become a testbed for the 3,000 lb Viper 20 engine and was given the pre-BAC designation Hunting H.166. With D. G. 'Dizzy' Addicott at the controls and Dave Crosser as observer, XS231 first flew from Luton on 16 March 1965. The aircraft performed well and, despite the extra power, handled no differently from a standard Jet Provost. Briefly redesignated the BAC 166, and briefly given the civilian registration G-ATAJ, the aircraft served in the flight evaluation role for another project, the BAC 167 Strikemaster. By now settled at Warton, XS231 was reconverted to become the second prototype T.5 and, in this guise, was first flown by Reg Stock and Malcolm Ribchester on 12 July 1967. Contract KC/E/124/CB5(b) was placed in July 1968 for 110 Jet Provost T.5s. The first production T.5, XW287, took to the air for the first time on 16 July 1969 and the first deliveries of the new mark were issued to the CFS on 3 September 1969.

Originally scheduled to be built as a Jet Provost T.4, XS230 was chosen instead as one of two T.5 prototypes. The aircraft is pictured at Warton in early 1967. (BAC via R. L. Ward Collection)

Prototype Jet Provost T.5P XS230 carried out its maiden flight on 28 February 1967 and enjoyed a long service career. It is one of several civilian examples still flying today. (R. L. Ward Collection)

The second prototype Jet Provost T.5, XS231, once again captured at the BAC airfield at Warton in Lancashire. Only the nose of this aircraft survives today at the Boscombe Down Aviation Collection. (BAC via R. L. Ward Collection)

Jet Provost T.5 XS231 in home territory off the Lancashire coast. (BAC (CN 737) via Martin Richmond Photos)

XS231 was destined to never enter RAF service but instead served as BAC 166 prototype with a Viper 20 engine and was then reconfigured to T.5 standard to serve in the flight evaluation and development role. (BAC via R. L. Ward Collection)

The Jet Provost
T.3 to T.5 in Service

Central Flying School (CFS)

The CFS, located at RAF Little Rissington, was the first RAF training unit to take delivery of the Jet Provost T.3 in July 1959. The aircraft, XM360, XM361 and XM365, were collected from RAF Lyneham by Flt Lts Norman Giffin, Fred Packer and Bert Cann. The first course, No. 199, to receive training on the Jet Provost ran between June and September 1959 and six of the thirteen students qualified as QFIs on type and were posted to No. 2 FTS.

The Jet Provost T.4 arrived on 23 November 1960, the first two aircraft being XP549 and XP550, followed the next month by XP551 and XP553. Thanks to the increased performance of the T.4, the flying training syllabus could be changed to include more higher altitude work. The first Jet Provost T.5, XW287, arrived at Little Rissington on 3 September 1969 and was delivered direct by BAC Senior Production Test Pilot 'Pete' Ginger. Because of the high workload placed upon the unpressurised T.4s, their service careers were short and the type was withdrawn from CFS from October 1969 onwards. The last T.4, XN467, left the CFS on 16 June 1970, bound for storage at No. 27 MU, RAF Shawbury.

The CFS stock of Jet Provosts recovered slightly between February and July 1974 when the unit took delivery of the Jet Provost T.3A and T.5A, modified and upgraded by BAC at Warton. The non-upgraded T.3s had all but departed Little Rissington by late 1975. However, Little Rissington's days were also numbered, the airfield being one of twelve that would be destined to close in the mid-1970s. The final Jet Provost course, No. 276, was concluded in April 1976, the CFS vacating to RAF Cranwell and being absorbed into the RAFC. Cranwell proved to be a busy airfield for the CFS and another move followed in September 1977, when the unit travelled further north to RAF Leeming, the home of No. 3 FTS. Once again, closure forced the CFS out, this time to RAF Scampton in 1984. It was here that the CFS's long association with the Jet Provost came to an end. The T.3As were phased out from 1989 and the T.5A in June 1992 to make way for the Tucano T.1.

No. 2 Flying Training School

Having successfully completed the 'Hullavington Experiment', No. 2 FTS was chosen as the first flying training school to be equipped with the Jet Provost T.3. By then, No. 2 FTS had relocated to RAF Syerston in November 1959, the unit having received its first T.3 on 20 August 1959. The first course, No. 143, began on 7 October 1959, by which time the unit had a dozen T.3s on strength. No. 2 FTS hosted several courses for foreign students, including pilots from Sudan and Kuwait, both of whom were destined to fly the armed export versions of the Jet Provost.

The first T.4s arrived at Syerston in May 1962; No. 155 Course, which had started the previous March, saw the new mark in. The late 1960s saw a major reorganisation of the RAF and one of the casualties would be No. 2 FTS, which was earmarked for closure in 1969. By the beginning of that year the Jet Provost T.3s were slowly transferred to other units, while the T.4s continued to the end. The final course, No. 183, began in February with eighteen students and was successfully completed on 19 December 1969. No. 2 FTS was disbanded on 16 January 1970, only to be reformed the same day as a Primary Flying School at RAF Church Fenton with Chipmunks; its Jet Provost days were over for good.

Royal Air Force College (RAFC)

A familiar sight from the nearby A17 for over three decades, the first Jet Provost to arrive at the RAFC, RAF Cranwell, near Sleaford in Lincolnshire was a T.3 in June 1960. The RAFC would later operate the T.4, the T.3A, T.5 and T.5A right up to the first Tucano delivery in June 1991. The final RAFC Jet Provost was sent to No. 1 FTS at RAF Linton-on-Ouse in December 1991.

No. 1 Flying Training School

No. 1 FTS was originally formed back in 1919 at Netheravon and as such is the world's oldest flying training school. The incarnation we are interested in was reformed at RAF Syerston on 1 May 1955 with Provosts, Chipmunks and Vampires before moving to RAF Linton-on-Ouse in November 1957. The main tasking for No. 1 FTS at the time was to provide initial flying training to potential FAA pilots; basic flying was carried out with the Provost and advanced with the Vampire.

The unit's first Jet Provost T.3, XM468, arrived in August 1960, No. 93 Course being the first, albeit with a mix of piston and Jet Provost. It was not until February 1961 that No. 1 FTS had enough T.3s to provide all-jet training, the piston-powered versions clinging on until July. The Jet Provost T.4 followed promptly, the first example, XP615, arriving on 27 April 1962. While FAA pilots were unaffected, with the conclusion of No. 9 (Linton) Course on 13 October 1964 advanced flying training on the Vampire came to an end for RAF pilots. *Ab initio* training for FAA fixed-wing pilots came to an end at Linton in July 1969. However, the previous year saw the re-introduction of basic flying training for RAF pilots and it was the latter which would now take up No. 1 FTS's time. The FAA were destined to return; those pilots creamed off to fly the Sea Harrier would be training on the Jet Provost before progressing.

The first Jet Provost T.5s arrived at Linton in December 1970, XW298 and XW299 being the first examples. The new type quickly replaced the T.4s, the last of them having departed by July 1970. From this point onwards, the T.3s were employed for basic training while the T.5s were used for 'Fast Jet Lead In', which effectively prepared the student for progression to the Gnat or Hawk. The T.3A and T.5A were introduced during the mid-1970s and it was with these two variants that No. 1 FTS would continue to fly through the 1980s and early 1990s. The beginning of the end for No. 1 FTS and the Jet Provost came in April 1992 when a Tucano T.1 was delivered to the school. The final Jet Provost course was No. 125, which concluded on 4 June 1993. On 22 July 1993, the OC of No. 1 FTS and Station Commander, Group Captain Tom Eeles, led a formation of five T.3As on a final flight to RAF Shawbury via Scampton, Cranwell and Brampton.

No. 6 Flying Training School

Another old flying training school that was first formed in April 1920 at Spittlegate, No. 6 FTS had just moved from RAF Ternhill to RAF Acklington when it received its first Jet Provost T.3 on 4 August 1961. The T.3 establishment rose quickly enough for the first course, No. 162, to commence with twenty-four students on 13 September 1961. The Jet Provost T.4 began to arrive in 1963 and with these two marks No. 6 FTS trained many RAF and overseas students before the final course, No. 184, was completed on 16 February 1968. Course No. 184 was also significant because the 1,000th student graduated from it before No. 6 FTS was disbanded on 30 June 1968. No. 6 FTS was a busy unit; during its tenure at Acklington it had trained 1,058 pilots and logged more than 100,000 flying hours – 211 of the latter being achieved in one day.

No. 6 FTS was reformed at RAF Finningley on 1 May 1970 as a Vickers Varsity T.1-equipped air navigation school. The unit was bolstered by a dozen Hawker Siddeley Dominie T.1s in August and, around the same time, took delivery of Jet Provost T.3s XM419, XN506 and XN509. The T.3s were used to train student navigators and the first course began in September. No. 6 FTS continued to grow as the year progressed and by the end of it had twenty Varsities, thirteen Dominies and seven Jet Provosts on strength.

The first examples of the faster Jet Provost T.4 arrived in March 1971, to be used for high-speed, low-level exercises. By 1974 the Varsities had gone without having a replacement, leaving the Dominie and Jet Provosts to soldier on. The situation was eased slightly with the introduction of one the rare marks of Jet Provost, the unofficially-designated T.5B. The T.5B had a greater range and endurance compared to a stock T.5 due to a pair of 48-gallon tip tanks. At least thirteen T.5Bs passed through No. 6 FTS, the type being first used as part of No. 6 Air Defence 'Lead-In' Course during November and December 1975.

By the late 1980s, the T.5Bs were becoming tired and were failing routine fatigue tests. As a result, five low hours T.5Bs were quickly modified with tip tanks at RAF Scampton and delivered to No. 6 FTS in November 1988. Government cutbacks began to take their toll in the early 1990s and it was announced that all navigator training would be carried out by No. 3 FTS at RAF Cranwell and that Finningley would be closed. As a result, the Jet Provosts were retired by No. 6 FTS on 14 August 1993 and later flown to RAF Shawbury for disposal. It was all over for No. 6 FTS on 31 March 1996.

No. 3 Flying Training School

No. 3 FTS was first formed back in April 1920 at RAF Waddington. It was the unit's fourth reincarnation following reformation on 15 September 1961. Located at RAF Leeming, the unit's first three Jet Provost T.3s were XN574, XN606 and XN629, all of which arrived on the formation day direct from Luton. The first course began in late October, but it was not until the end of December 1961 that the unit was up to full T.3 strength with twenty-four aircraft. At first the course length was thirty-six weeks long and would include 120 flying hours. However, by early 1962 this was revised and increased to a forty-eight-week-long course with 160 flying hours. The new course would commence on the T.3, with advanced flying on the Jet Provost T.4, the first of which arrived on 21 March 1962.

The first T.5 for No. 3 FTS was XW315, which arrived on 17 July 1970; the total had increased to seventeen T.5s by the end of the year, which allowed the T.4 to be phased out. No. 3 FTS soaked up the School of Refresher Training from Manby in December 1973 but sadly the writing was on the wall for the unit. A reduction in pilot training took its toll across the RAF, but No. 3 FTS soldiered on, still absorbing the Royal Navy EFTS from Church Fenton in November 1974.

No. 3 FTS was disbanded on 26 April 1984, its aircraft were transferred to the CFS and RAF Leeming was closed. However, No. 3 FTS was resurrected on 1 February 1989 from a flying element of the RAF College at RAF Cranwell for *ab initio* training of RAF pilots after their officer training. They were equipped with Jet Provost T.5A, which remained there until 29 October 1991.

No. 7 (Basic) Flying Training School

Reformed at RAF Church Fenton on 13 March 1962 with the Jet Provost T.3, No. 7 FTS inaugural *ab initio* course, with twenty-six students, began on 23 April. The T.4 began to arrive in 1963, but No. 7 FTS's tenure was destined to be short. The final course, No. 17 – made up of seventeen students, three of whom were from the Jordanian Air Force – concluded on 17 November 1965. Disbanded on 30 November 1966, it was not quite all over for No. 7 FTS, which was reformed again on 2 April 1979 because of the shortage of pilots for the Panavia Tornado. Again operating from Church Fenton, the unit was initially equipped with the Jet Provost T.3A, the first of them, XM376, XM475, XN473 and XN604, arriving on formation day from Cranwell. More aircraft arrived later in April in the shape of the Jet Provost T.5A, the first examples being XW371, XW372, XW417 and XW419. The number of aircraft increased dramatically during the 1980s but the arrival of the RAF's first Tucano T.1 in 1989 sounded the beginning of the end for the Jet Provost. Most aircraft were transferred to other units and the last of them, a T.5A, departed in September 1991. No. 7 FTS was disbanded on 31 March 1992.

RAF College of Air Warfare (CAW)/School of Refresher Flying (SoRF)

The RAF CAW was formed on 1 July 1962 by renaming the RAFC at RAF Manby, to teach new techniques and tactics and give refresher training. The CAW was equipped with a wide range of service types. The jet types, such as the Gloster Meteor and English Electric Canberra, which were operated by the CAW were flown from Manby's satellite at Strubby where No. 3 All Weather Jet Refresher Squadron (AWJFS) restored pilots' handling skills. Following another reorganisation, the AWJFS became the School of Refresher Training (SoRF) in July 1962 and, in February 1964, the unit's Meteors (T.7s and F.8s) were replaced with Jet Provost T.4s, XS186, XS209 and XS210 being delivered first.

On 3 December 1973, it was all change again; the SoRF was moved to RAF Leeming to become part of No. 3 FTS, specifically renamed '1 Sqn/3 FTS'. Renamed again in 1977 as the Refresher Flying Squadron, the unit remained at Leeming until 1984, when it was moved to RAF Church Fenton to operate alongside the resident No. 7 FTS. The end for CAW was more clinical and the unit transferred its tasking to the RAFC, Cranwell, on 7 January 1974 to become the Department of Air Warfare.

Jet Provost Trials Unit

The JPTU was formed on 4 September 1965 at RAF Tengah with three Jet Provost T.4s. The unit was attached to No. 20 Squadron (Hunters), remaining active until 14 March 1966.

Central Air Traffic Control School

Formed at RAF Shawbury on 11 February 1963, the Central Air Traffic Control (CATCS), was originally equipped with the Provost T.1 and Vampire T.11. The first Jet Provost T.4 did not arrive until 1973, the type having been withdrawn from the majority of flying training schools. A large number of T.4s passed through the school, the type serving as a 'live' training aid for junior air traffic controllers. CATCS was the last RAF unit to operate the T.4, which was retired in July 1989.

No. 26 Squadron

Reformed as a holding unit for the personnel at HQ, Training Command, RAF Brampton, No. 26 Squadron took delivery of its first two Jet Provost T.3s in July 1974. Operating from RAF Wyton, the unit was renamed the 'Wyton Detachment' on 31 March 1976 and on 31 December 1976 was transferred to the RAFC and renamed again as the 'Jet Provost Detachment'. The detachment operated until October 1977.

Tactical Weapons Unit and No. 1 Tactical Weapons Unit

The Tactical Weapons Unit (TWU) was formed on 2 September 1974 from part of No. 229 OCU at RAF Brawdy, complete with Nos 63, 79 and 234 Shadow Squadrons. The TWU came about because of the disbandment of No. 229 OCU at RAF Chivenor, which operated many Hawker Hunters. The OCU had a large number of support aircraft which included at least three Jet Provost T.3s – XM475 'F', XN579 and XN584. These aircraft served with a Standards Flight in support of RAF and Army Forward Air Controllers, operating with the Joint Forward Air Control Training and Standards Unit (JAFACTSU). Under the control of the TWU, the unit was set to gain more Jet Provosts, this time several T.4s, the T.3s having already found new homes.

The CFS Aerobatic Team of the 1960 season were four Jet Provost T.3s: XM355, XM357, XM360 and XM361. The team are performing at Yeadon (today Leeds/Bradford Airport) on 6 June 1960. (R. L. Ward)

In order for the RAF to gain a second TWU the unit was renamed No. 1 TWU on 31 July 1978, while the second unit, No. 2 TWU, also operating the Hunter and later the Hawk, was formed at RAF Lossiemouth the same day. No. 2 TWU also had at least one Jet Provost in the support role including T.3 XM378, while No. 1 TWU is credited with having at least four on strength at any one time, although at least eight aircraft passed through the unit. No. 1 TWU's Jet Provosts were the only RAF examples to be painted in full camouflage.

Above: One of the first Jet Provost T.3s to be delivered to the CFS at RAF Little Rissington was XM360 '71'. This aircraft was lost on 24 January 1969 when it crashed into Brown Clee Hill, Abdon, Shropshire. (R. L. Ward Collection)

Below: An impressive formation by five Jet Provost T.4s of the CFS, RAF Little Rissington, *c.* 1962. (R. L. Ward Collection)

Above: Delivered to CFS on 7 December 1961, Jet Provost T.4 XP552 remained at Little Rissington until 16 May 1966, when the aircraft was transferred to No. 3 FTS. (R. L. Ward Collection)

Below: The CFS display team evolved into the 'Red Pelicans' from 1962 through to 1973. The team was made up of four Jet Provost T.5s from 1969, the first aircraft being XW287, which is pictured leading this formation. (MoD/Crown Copyright (TN6729/56) via R. L. Ward Collection)

Above: The striking all-red scheme (slightly lost in this black and white photo!) of the CFS 'Red Pelican' display team pictured over BAC Warton with their Jet Provost T.4s. (BAC (AW FA483) via Martin Richmond Photos)

Below: Jet Provost T.1s of No. 2 FTS tucked up tight during the 'Hullavington Experiment', the successful outcome of which endorsed the aircraft as the future RAF basic jet trainer. (R. L. Ward Collection)

Above: Jet Provost T.3 XM420 '44' of No. 2 FTS taxiing out for take-off at RAF Woodvale on 25 June 1960. (R. L. Ward)

Below: There was no shortage of RAF air shows to attend during the 1960s and No. 2 FTS contributed to a great number of them. This is Jet Provost T.3 '32' of No. 2 FTS at RAF Wethersfield on 17 June 1961. (R. L. Ward)

Above: Jet Provost T.3 XN636 '58' of the RAF College on finals into RAF Cranwell. (R. L. Ward Collection)

Below: The RAF College's first display was the 'Cranwell Poachers', which displayed in 1965 and then made a return between 1968 and 1970. The team was renamed 'The Poachers' and continued to perform until 1976. (MoD/Crown Copyright (TN6534/77) via R. L. Ward Collection)

Above: A typically busy scene at RAF Cranwell, with one of the RAF College's 'The Poachers' display team Jet Provost T.5s taxiing in the foreground. Behind is a range of T.3s, T.4s and T.5s of the RAFC and CFS captured on 24 June 1976. (J. D. R. Rawlings via R. L. Ward Collection)

Below: Long-serving Jet Provost T.3As XM466 and XM424 of No. 1 FTS still look great after more than thirty years of RAF service. (Crown Copyright via R. L. Ward Collection)

Above: Another view of No. 1 FTS T.3A XM466 in her final, impressive colour scheme before retirement from the RAF in 1993. (Crown Copyright via R. L. Ward Collection)

Below: Jet Provost T.5 XW308 '67' of No. 1 FTS at RAF Linton-on-Ouse, 12 August 1970. Later converted to T.5A standard, the aircraft was lost on 28 October 1981 when it crashed after take-off near RAF Leuchars. (R. L. Ward)

Above: No. 1 FTS had three display teams between 1963 and 1973. The last was called the 'Linton Blades' and they are pictured here over a snow-covered Yorkshire in 1973. (Crown Copyright via R. L. Ward Collection)

Right: A quartet of No. 1 FTS Jet Provost T.5s out of RAF Linton-on-Ouse bank over RAF Fylingdales on the North Yorkshire Moors. (BAC (CN 737) via Martin Richmond Photos)

Above: Delivered to No. 6 FTS at RAF Acklington on 14 December 1961, T.3 XM474 '17' was a troublesome aircraft for the unit. The Jet Provost was declared 'rogue' as a result of spinning problems. (R. L. Ward Collection)

Below: Jet Provost T.4 XP662 '45' of No. 6 FTS on a visit to RAF Stradishall on 4 October 1964. (R. L. Ward)

One of thirteen conversions, this is Jet Provost T.5B XW306 of No. 6 FTS on the flight line at Yeovilton on 3 September 1977. A No. 1 Squadron Hawker Siddeley Harrier GR.3 is parked beyond. (R. L. Ward)

The Jet Provost was not a common sight in RAF Germany, making this No. 3 FTS Jet Provost T.4, XR651 '53', at RAF Wildenrath on 4 July 1970 unusual. (R. L. Ward)

Jet Provost T.5A XW429 '57' of No. 3 FTS closes in on the 'camera ship' c. 1976/77. (Crown Copyright via Chris Hearn)

The first of two No. 3 FTS display teams was the 'Gemini Pair' comprising two Jet Provost T.4s during the 1970 season and, as seen here, two T.5s from 1971 to 1973. (MoD/ Crown Copyright (TM 6474/57) via R. L. Ward Collection)

The 'Gemini Pair' during a performance at RAF Chivenor on 5 August 1972. (R. L. Ward)

The second No. 3 FTS display team, named 'The Swords', appeared for the 1974 display season and was made up of four Jet Provost T.5s, including XW370. (R. L. Ward Collection)

'The Swords' display team line-up for the 1974 and last display season was (Left to Right); Flt John Aldington (No. 2); Flt Lt Bob Thompson (No. 1); Flt Lt Dick Thomas (No. 4); and Flt Lt Mike Fox (No. 3). (RAF Command Public Relations Staff Photo via R. L. Ward Collection)

Jet Provost T.3 XM410 '48' joined No. 7 FTS at RAF Church Fenton on 4 September 1962 and was transferred to the RAFC on 21 April 1966. (R. L. Ward Collection)

Another Jet Provost T.3 which served with No. 7 FTS during its first *ab initio* period was XM413 '25', which served from 21 March 1962 until 30 June 1966, when the aircraft was transferred to No. 2 FTS. (R. L. Ward Collection)

Above: Delivered to No. 7 FTS from No. 27 MU, RAF Shawbury, on 16 January 1964, Jet Provost T.4 XS175 'X' was returned to No. 27 MU on 9 December 1966. (R. L. Ward Collection)

Below: Between 1979 and 1991, No. 7 FTS operated a number of Jet Provost T.5As including XW373 '121/CF' pictured at Fairford on 13 July 1985. (R. L. Ward Collection)

Above: No. 7 FTS Jet Provost T.3A XN590 '86', which was delivered to the Church Fenton-based unit on 29 March 1979. The aircraft crashed at RAF Elvington following multiple bird strikes on 31 July 1980. (MoD/Crown Copyright (TN6546/21) via (R. L. Ward Collection)

Below: Some of CAW's newly arrived Jet Provost T.4s present themselves to the camera over Lincolnshire in the mid-1960s. (MoD (PRB (AIR) 35485) via R. L. Ward Collection)

Originally named 'The Magistrates', the CAW's display team was renamed the 'The Macaws' in late 1967 and performed in the UK and across Europe until 1973. (MoD (PRB (AIR)) via R. L. Ward Collection)

The full camouflage gives this Jet Provost away as a No. 1 TWU machine – specifically XP547 '03', pictured at RAF Abingdon on 10 September 1983. (R. L. Ward)

XP547 approaching the end of her flying career and now painted in low-visibility grey. The aircraft is seen on the static line at Fairford on 18 July 1987. (R. L. Ward Collection)

Export Variants

T.51

Despite the fact that the standard RAF Jet Provost T.3 was not required to carry out weapons training during its career, the manufacturers had the foresight to incorporate certain features so that it could. Space for machine guns and hard points under the wings for both rockets and bombs gave the manufacturers the opportunity to present an armed export version, the first of which was designated as the T.51.

Internally, the weapons fit, included a pair of .303 inch (7.7 mm) machine guns in each wing root with space for 500 rounds of ammunition backed up with a reflector gun sight in the cockpit plus a gun camera in the nose. External weaponry carried under the wings included a combination of the following: up to eight 25 lb fragmentation bombs on standard bomb racks, six Mk 8 rockets with 60 lb heads, a dozen Mk 5 rockets, eight 25 lb fragmentation bombs and four Mk 8 rockets or eight 25 lb fragmentation bombs and eight Mk 5 rockets.

A total of twenty-two T.51s were sold as primary/weapons trainers, although the type obviously had a more hostile ground attack capability. The first order was placed by the Ceylon Air Force, comprising a dozen aircraft serialled CJ701–712; these were delivered between December 1959 and December 1960. The first of the batch was actually the hard-working T.2 G-23-1, which was converted to T.51 standard and delivered to Ceylon on 13 December 1959; serialled CJ701, the Jet Provost is one of several preserved in Sri Lanka today.

The Sudanese Air Force was the next overseas customer, taking delivery of all four of its T.51s on 17 October 1961. Serialled 124, 139, 143 and 157, the first two aircraft had short careers, both being written off on 26 May (139) and 13 June 1962 (124), while the other two aircraft were returned to BAC, refurbished, and sold on to the Nigerian Air Force in August 1967. Re-serialled NAF701 and NAF702, very little is known about their flying careers other than the fact that the former made a forced landing near Porto Novo on 23 June 1969 without injury to the crew and with little damage to the aircraft.

The final purchaser of the T.51 was the Kuwait Air Force, who ordered half a dozen, serialled 101–106. Delivered in early 1962, all were withdrawn from use by 1970 and at least five of the six aircraft survive in store as part of the Kuwait Air Force Collection, located at the country's international airport.

T.52

Basically the armed export version of the Jet Provost T.4, the T.52 was marginally more successful from an overseas sales point of view. The first customer was the Sudanese Air Force, who ordered eight aircraft serialled 162, 173, 175, 180, 181, 185, 190 and 195. Delivery took place between 28 November 1962 and 27 January 1964. T.52 '181', an aircraft originally intended for the Venezuelan Air Force, was the only loss from this batch of aircraft, the Jet Provost force landing near Idididje on 7 April 1964 during a ferry flight from Fort Lamy to Sudan.

Venezuela was the next air force to order the T.52, fifteen of them in total being serialled E-040 to E-054, and all delivered in February 1963. However, their service careers appear to have been quite short and all were either grounded or had been placed into storage by 1966.

The Iraqi Air Force was the next customer, purchasing twenty T.52s serialled 600 to 619, with delivery taking place between 31 August 1964 and 28 April 1965. It is not clear how long the Iraqis kept their T.52s in service but all twenty were still on the inventory prior to the first Gulf War in 1990 and, considering the destruction wreaked during that conflict, it is impressive that only five had been destroyed by the end. It is believed that the majority, if not all fifteen remaining airframes still survive in varying states of repair.

With overseas sales of the Jet Provost T.52 appearing to dry up post-1965, an order from the South Yemini Air Force kept the breed alive. However, these would not be 'new-build' aircraft but ex-RAF machines, albeit two of them having served with a training establishment including the Jet Provost Trials Unit, Nos 3, 6 and 7 FTSs. Eight aircraft were ordered and the following aircraft were selected for refurbishment and conversion to T.52A standard. The ex-RAF aircraft were XP666, XP684, XR652, XR661, XS223, XS224, XS227 and XS228, all of which were sold back to BAC between 13 January and 30 August 1967. The conversion work was subcontracted to Marshall's of Cambridge and the aircraft, re-serialled 101 to 108, were delivered to Yemen between 12 October 1967 and 31 January 1968. Once again service career information is sketchy, but it is known that '103' (ex-XS227) was the only aircraft of the batch to be written off. It is also known that at least five of these aircraft were sold on to the Singapore Air Force in 1975 (complete with ex-XN596, supplied by BAC as an instructional airframe) and the type remained in service until 1980.

A potentially very large order from the South African Air Force for the T.52 was scuppered by the Labour Government's block on armament exports to that country and, like the RAAF, the SAAF equipped with the Macchi MB.326 instead.

T.55

The final export version of the Jet Provost was the T.55, the armed equivalent of the RAF's T.5. The customer was again the Sudan Air Force, who ordered five aircraft serialled 167, 177, 187, 192 and 197. Delivery took place on 30 March (three aircraft) and 13 June 1969 (two aircraft). Again, the service careers of these aircraft is not fully clear but it was reported in a 1990 edition of *Flight* that three T.55s remained on strength, operating in company with a trio of Strikemaster Mk.90s in the COIN role. The only other order placed for the T.55 was by the Greek Air Force, but unfortunately this was also embargoed by the Labour Government in 1974.

Above: Ceylon Air Force Jet Provost T.51 CJ701 (ex-T.2, G-23-1) captured prior to delivery in 1959. (Hunting Group via R. L. Ward Collection)

Below: A close up of the underwing weapons carried by CJ701 during a demonstration flight – in this case, eight 25 lb fragmentation bombs and four Mk 8 rockets per side. (Hunting Group via R. L. Ward Collection)

Above: Ex-Ceylon Air Force Jet Provost T.51 CJ711, one of several surviving examples. The aircraft is preserved at the Sri Lanka Air Force Museum at Ratmalana. (R. L. Ward Collection)

Below: The first of four Jet Provost T.51s, ordered by the Sudanese Air Force in 1961. '124' had a short flying career, the aircraft being written off in a landing accident on 13 June 1962. (Hunting Group via R. L. Ward Collection)

Above: The first of fifteen Jet Provost T.52s ordered for the Venezuelan Air Force, 'E-040' is pictured in early 1963. (Hunting Group via R. L. Ward Collection)

Below: The second of twenty Jet Provost T.52s ordered for the Iraqi Air Force, '601' was delivered on 31 August 1964. (R. L. Ward Collection)

59

Above: Iraqi Air Force Jet Provost T.52 '603' at Farnborough in September 1964; the aircraft was delivered the following month. (R. L. Ward Collection)

Below: One of the eight Jet Provost T.52As for the South Yemen Air Force. (R. L. Ward Collection)

Above: Ex-T.4 XS228 was converted to a T.52A for South Yemen and serialled '103'. After service with the Singapore Air Force, the aircraft was sold and flown on the civilian register as G-PROV. The aircraft still flies and today has returned to its original South Yemen Air Force appearance. (R. L. Ward Collection)

Below: The final export variant of the Jet Provost was the T.55. '167' was the first of only five aircraft for the Sudanese Air Force. (R. L. Ward Collection)

Strikemaster

A development of the Jet Provost T.5, the Hunting H.167, later the BAC 167, was created in response to an overseas requirement for a light attack aircraft which could serve in the Counter-Insurgency (COIN) role. As already mentioned, the idea of an armed version of the Jet Provost was on the table very early on in the aircraft's development, the T.51, 52 and 55 variants being the first examples of this concept. Creating a more dedicated military variant of the Jet Provost would also keep the type in production beyond the RAF orders and BAC had high hopes that the new aircraft, later named the Strikemaster, would appeal to many smaller overseas air forces.

The most significant feature of the BAC 167 was the powerplant, a 3,410 lb Viper 535 (20F20) which gave the aircraft the extra grunt it needed in hot/high environments, not to mention surplus power for a potentially large amount of underwing stores. To cope with these stores, the aircraft's stress load was increased up to 3,100 lb and spread across four underwing pylons. The range of weapons of the BAC 167 was impressive and included a quartet of 75-gallon fuel tanks, four conventional 500 lb bombs, two dozen Oerlikon-Bührle SURA R80 rockets, eight 20 lb fragmentation or eight 25 lb practice bombs, four SNEB pods each with eighteen 68 mm unguided air-to-ground RPs or a pair of 0.5 inch mini-gun pods. Internally, a pair of 7.62 mm Fraser-Nash machine guns was installed, complete with 600 rounds of ammunition. Other options included the fitment of a Vinten G90 gun camera in the nose and in the cockpit, a Ferranti LFS 5, GM 2 reflector or SFOM gun sight.

Fuel capacity of the BAC 167 was a total of 270 gallons, made up of 48 gallons in each wing tip, which now had conformal-type tanks, while the remainder was carried by internal bag-type tanks in both in the inner and outer wings. The original robust undercarriage of the Jet Provost was retained as rig testing did not foresee any structural problems attributable to the extra weight imposed by the stores load. The all-up weight of the aircraft increased from the T.5's 9,200 lb to the BAC 167's 11,500 lb's, but this made little difference, stress-wise, to the airframe.

The prototype BAC 167, serialled G-27-8, made its maiden flight with Reg Stock at the controls from Warton on 26 October 1967. All was looking rosy for the Strikemaster (officially named in October 1968) with a substantial pre-order for the aircraft placed by Saudi Arabia in December 1965. In typical Saudi fashion, a complete air-defence bundle was purchased, comprising twenty-five aircraft and valued at over £100 million. The first aircraft, designated as the Strikemaster Mk 80, were delivered to the King Faisal Air Academy (a military flight school) at Riyadh in September 1969. This order would prove to be the largest single purchase of the aircraft, but other orders would follow in quick succession including a further twenty aircraft, the Strikemaster Mk 80A, again for Saudi Arabia. Other orders included four Mk 81s for South Yemen (renamed the People's Republic of Yemen Air Force post-delivery), a dozen Mk 82s and a further dozen Mk 82As for Oman, a dozen Mk 83s for Kuwait, sixteen Mk 84s for Singapore, six Mk 87s for Kenya, sixteen Mk 88s for New Zealand and twenty-two Mk 89s for Ecuador. Out of this group, aircraft of South Yemen, Oman and Ecuador were used in action; Oman during the long Dhofar Rebellion and more recently by Ecuador during the Cenepar War during January and February 1995 over a border dispute with Peru.

Production of the Strikemaster was concluded at Warton by mid-1978, the company turning its focus onto the manufacture of the Sepecat Jaguar. However, it was not quite over for the Strikemaster as BAC decided to shift production to Hurn, which was the main producer of Jet Provost wings from 1966. Work was lacking at Hurn following the completion of all BAC One Eleven contracts, so the arrival of the first Strikemaster fuselage from Warton in November 1979 was appreciated by the workforce. Operating a final assembly line, the first Hurn-built aircraft was G16-26, which first flew from the Dorset airfield on 7 August 1980. The aircraft was registered as G-BIDB and, along with a second aircraft, G16-27, registered as G-BIHZ, served as a company demonstration aircraft. The aircraft were on display at the Farnborough and Paris air shows and in May 1981 they both paid a visit to Khartoum to take part in the Sudan Armed Forces Day. It was looking like the end for the Strikemaster but the visit to Sudan did finally pay off in 1983 when the country agreed a deal to purchase all of the remaining aircraft at Hurn. However, only three, which had first flown in 1980, were delivered in November 1983 before another arms embargo was enforced. The closure of the Hurn site in May 1984 saw three Strikemasters flying back to Warton and a further four uncompleted aircraft returning to Lancashire by road. This final batch of seven Strikemasters was eventually purchased: one by Sudan in September 1986 and the remainder by Ecuador, the last example serialled FAE261-264 on 21 October 1988.

Only one country purchased the Strikemaster second-hand, namely the Botswana Defence Force who acquired three ex-Kuwaiti Air Force Mk 83s and three ex-Kenyan Air Force Mk 87s. The first three were delivered in April 1988, the second batch following in 1989. The type remained in BDF service until 1996, when they were replaced by thirteen Canadair CF-116s.

The second Strikemaster to be built, Mk 80 G29-9 (G-AWOR), was destined to serve the Royal Saudi Air Force with the serial '902'. (BAC via R. L. Ward Collection)

Above: Farnborough is always a great venue to show off your aircraft's capability, including the vast weapons range of this Strikemaster Mk 80A in 1976. Displaying its civilian serial G-BECI and its future Royal Saudi Air Force serial of '1124', the aircraft was delivered straight after the SBAC. (R. L. Ward Collection)

Below: RSAF Strikemaster Mk 80A 1133 (G-BESY) arriving at the Paris Air Show in June 1977. WFU in 1997, the aircraft has been preserved at IWM, Duxford, since 2002. (R. L. Ward)

Above: Royal Air Force of Oman Strikemaster Mk 82 '402', one of twenty-four aircraft ordered in 1969. (R. L. Ward Collection)

Below: Strikemaster Mk 82A of the RAF of Oman at Masirah in November 1991. (P. J. Cooper via R. L. Ward Collection)

Above: A Republic of Singapore Air Force Strikemaster Mk 84 captured during a pre-delivery sortie. (BAC (FA.532) via R. L. Ward Collection)

Below: Demonstrator Strikemaster Mk 84 G-AYHS '314' taxiing in at Farnborough on 7 September 1970. The aircraft was delivered to the Republic of Singapore Air Force on 28 September. (R. L. Ward)

Also serving as a demonstrator at the SBAC, Farnborough, in September 1970 was Strikemaster Mk 84 G-AYHT '315' on the static line, fronted by an impressive array of weapons. (R. L. Ward)

Strikemaster Mk 88 G-ZXK/NZ6364 being put through its paces during the 1972 SBAC, Farnborough. The RNZAF ordered sixteen Mk 88s, which served from 1972 until 1992. (R. L. Ward)

RNZAF Strikemaster Mk 88 on the left and Jet Provost T.5 on the right at the SBAC, Farnborough, September 1972. Their roles are clearly defined. (R. L. Ward)

Technical Specifications

T.1

Serials: G-AOBU, XD674–XD680, XD692–XD694 and one airframe for structural testing (x12) (Contract 6/Acft/9265)
Engine: One 1,640 lb Armstrong Siddeley Viper 102 (ASV.5) turbojet
Dimensions: Span, 35 ft 5 in; Length, 31 ft 11 in; Height, 12 ft 8 in
Weights: Max AUW, 6,750 lb
Performance: Max speed, 330 mph at 20,000 ft; Range, 492 miles; Service Ceiling, 31,000 ft; Climb Rate to 30,000 ft, 24.4 minutes

T.2

Serials: XD674 (converted), G-AOHD, G-23-1 (later T.3 prototype) and G-AOUS (x4)
Engine: One 1,750 lb Armstrong Siddeley Viper 102 (ASV.8) turbojet
Dimensions: Span, 35 ft 2 in; Length, 31 ft 10 in; Height, 10 ft 2 in
Weights: Max AUW, 6,830 lb
Performance: Max speed, 330 mph; Range, 680 miles; Service Ceiling, 31,000 ft; Climb Rate to 30,000 ft, 21 minutes

T.3 & T.3A*

Serials: XN117 (ex-T.2 G-23-1), XN137 (Contract 6/Acft/14157) to replace XM348, XN458–XN512, XN547–XN559, XN573–XN607 and XN629–XN643 (Contract KC/E/301 (x100))
Engine: One 1,750 lb Armstrong Siddeley Viper 102 (ASV.8) turbojet
Dimensions: Span, 36 ft 11 in (over tip tanks); Length, 32 ft 5 in; Height, 10 ft 2 in
Weights: Max AUW, 7,092 lb
Performance: Max speed, 326 mph; Range, 565 miles; Service Ceiling, 33,000 ft; Climb Rate to 30,000 ft, 21 minutes

*70 T.3 aircraft modified with improved avionics

T.4

Serials: XP547–XP589, XP614–XP642 and XP661–XP688 (Contract KC/E/041 (x100)); XR643–XR681 and XR697–XR707 (Contract KC/E/057 (x50)); XS175–XS186 and XS209–XS231 (Contract KC/E/070 (x35))
Engine: One 2,500 lb Armstrong Siddeley Viper 102 (ASV.11) turbojet
Dimensions: Span, 36 ft 11 in (over tip tanks); Length, 32 ft 5 in; Height, 10 ft 2 in
Weights: Max AUW, 7,400 lb
Performance: Max speed, 410 mph; Range, 600 miles; Service Ceiling, 31,000 ft; Climb Rate to 30,000 ft, 15 minutes

T.5

Serials: XW287–XW336, XW351–XW375 and XW404–XW438 (Contract KC/E/124 (x110))
Engine: One 2,500 lb Armstrong Siddeley Viper 102 (ASV.11) turbojet
Dimensions: Span, 35 ft 4 in; Length, 33 ft 7½ in; Height, 10 ft 2 in; Wing Area, 213.7 sq/ft
Weights: Max AUW, 9,200 lb
Performance: Max speed, 409 mph; Range, 900 miles; Service Ceiling, 36,700 ft

T.5A & T.5B*

Serials: XW288–290, 292, 294, 295, 299, 301, 303, 305, 308, 310, 312–323, 325–330, 332–336, 351, 353–355, 357–375, 404–438 (x93)
Engine: One 2,500 lb Bristol Siddeley Viper 201 turbojet
Dimensions: Span, 35 ft 4 in (36 ft 11 in with tip tanks); Length, 33 ft 7½ in; Height, 10 ft 2 in
Weights: Loaded with tip tanks, 9,200 lbs
Performance: Max level speed, 409 mph at sea level; 440 mph at 25,000 ft; Initial Climb Rate, 3,550 ft/min; Range, 900 miles; Service Ceiling, 36,700 ft

*13 aircraft were fitted with tip-tanks and employed as navigational trainers under this designation

T.51 (Spec as per T.3)

Serials: CJ701–712 (Ceylon); 124, 139, 143 and 157 (Sudan); 101–106 (Kuwait)
Armament: Two 7.7mm (0.303 in) Mk 55 machine guns. External, a combination of up to eight 25 lb fragmentation bombs on standard bomb racks; six Mk 8 rockets with 60 lb heads; a dozen Mk 5 rockets; eight 25 lb fragmentation bombs and four Mk 8 rockets or eight 25 lb fragmentation bombs and eight Mk 5 rockets.

T.52 (Spec as per T.4)

Serials: 600–619 (Iraq); E–040–E–054 (Venezuela); 162, 173, 175, 180, 181, 185, 190 and 195 (Sudan)
Armament: As per T.51

T.55 (Spec as per T.5)

Serials: 167, 177, 187, 192 and 197 (Sudan)
Armament: As per T.51

Strikemaster Mk 80/80A/81/82/82A/83/84/87/88/89

Serials (in production order: (Warton) – Mk 80, 901–912 and 1101–1113 (Saudi Arabia); Mk 81, 501–504 (South Yemen) Mk 82, 401–407 (Oman); Mk 84, 300–315 (Singapore); Mk 82, 408–412 (Oman); Mk 83, 110–115 (Kuwait); Mk 87, 601–606 (Kenya); Mk 83, 116–121 (Kuwait); Mk 88, NZ6361–6370 (New Zealand); Mk 89, 243–250 (Ecuador); Mk 82A, 413–420 (Oman); Mk 80A, 1114–1123 (Saudi Arabia); Mk 89, 251–254 (Ecuador); Mk 88, NZ6371–6376 (New Zealand); Mk 82A, 421–424 (Oman); Mk 89, 255–258 (Ecuador); Mk 80A, 1124–1135 (Saudi Arabia).
(Hurn – final assembly) – Mk 89, 259–260 (Ecuador); Mk 90, 141, 142 and 144 (Sudan); Mk 89, 261–264 (Ecuador); Mk 80A, 425 (Oman).
Engine: One 3,410 lb Rolls-Royce Viper 535 (20F-20) turbojet
Dimensions: Span, 36 ft 11 in (over tip tanks); Length, 33 ft 7½ in; Height, 10 ft 2 in
Weights: Max AUW, 11,500 lbs
Performance: Max speed, 450 mph; Max ferry range with a 3,100 lb load, 1,450 miles; Service Ceiling, 31,000 ft
Armament: Two 7.62 mm Fraser-Nash machines. Multiple options including – four 75-gallon fuel tanks, four 500 lb bombs, twenty-four SURA R80 rockets, eight 25 lb practice bombs or 20 lb fragmentation bombs, four eighteen-tube SNEB 68 mm rockets or two 0.5 inch mini-gun pods.

RAF Jet Provost Units and Operators

Central Flying School *Imprimis Praecepta (Our teaching is everlasting)*

A/c   All marks (except T.2)
Dates   31 August 1959 to 1992
Stations   Little Rissington, Cranwell, Leeming and Scampton
A/c: *T.1*, XD675–680, XD693; *T.3*, XM346, XM349, XM355–361, XM364, XM366, XM371, XM374–375, XM378, XM386–387, XM401, XM403, XM411, XM413, XM418–419, XM422–426, XM428, XM453, XM455, XM458–461, XM466, XM470–74, XN137, XN459, XN462, XN464–465, XN467–468, XN472, XN499, XN501–502, XN506, XN508, XN511–512, XN548–552, XN554, XN557, XN573, XN576, XN581, XN584, XN586, XN591, XN595, XN605, XN629, XN640, XN643; *T.4*, XP549–554, XP570–573, XP575, XP588, XP632, XP639–642, XP675, XP679, XR670–671, XR678, XR680, XR704–706, XS175, XS178, XS182, XS212–213, XS222, XS225–226, XS229; *T.5*, XW287–295, XW297, XW315–316, XW319, XW326–327, XW330, XW333, XW336, XW353, XW358, XW364, XW368, XW375, XW414–415, XW418–419, XW421, XW425, XW427, XW429–431, XW434–437.

CFS Jet Provost T.1s departing RAF Hucknall on 18 May 1959. (R. L. Ward)

Above: CFS Jet
Provost T.3 XM473 '61'
undergoing servicing at
RAF Little Rissington.
(R. L. Ward Collection)

Left: A quartet of CFS
Jet Provost T.3s about to
go over the top, *c.* 1960.
(Hunting Group via
R. L. Ward Collection)

CFS Jet Provost T.5A XW434 '92' on final approach into RAF Cranwell on 23 June 1976. (R. L. Ward)

No. 1 Flying Training School
Terra Marique ad Caelum (By Land and Sea to the Sky)

A/c	T.3, 3A, 4 and 5
Dates	August 1960 to July 1993
Station	Linton-on-Ouse

A/c: *T.3*, XM349–352, XM354–355, XM357–358, XM365, XM370, XM372, XM374, XM376, XM378, XM383, XM401, XM403, XM405, XM412, XM414, XM424–425, XM455, XM457–458, XM461, XM463–473, XM477–480, XN458–459, XN461–462, XN466, XN468–472, XN494–495, XN497–502, XN504–511, XN547, XN549, XN551–553, XN556, XN573–575, XN577, XN579, XN582, XN585–586, XN588–589, XN591–593, XN595, XN598, XN605–606, XN629–630, XN634, XN636, XN641, XN643; *T.4*, XP561, XP573, XP580, XP589, XP615–616, XP621, XP626–627, XP633–634, XP637, XP662, XP668, XP671, XP678–679, XP681, XP683, XR655, XR657, XR665–666, XR668, XR670, XR672, XR674, XR699–701, XS225; *T.5*, XW288– 289, XW294–313, XW317–328, XW330, XW333–334, XW336, XW351, XW354, XW359–361, XW363–372, XW374, XW404–405, XW408–410, XW412–413, XW415–417, XW419–420, XW423–424, XW426–430, XW432, XW434, XW436–437.

Above: No. 1 FTS 'Linton Gin' display team on the grass during an air show at Wycombe Air Park on 12 July 1969. (R. L. Ward)

Below: A pair of No. 1 FTS Jet Provost T.5s on the flight line at RAF Lakenheath on 2 August 1975. (R. L. Ward)

No. 2 Flying Training School

Verbum sat Sapienti (A Word to the Wise is Sufficient)

A/c	T.1, 2, 3 and 4
Dates	August 1955 to January 1970
Stations	Hullavington, Syerston

A/c: *T.1*, XD675–693; *T.2*, XD694; *T.3*, XM347, XM349, XM351, XM354, XM358–359, XM362–387, XM401–410, XM412–XM422, XM426, XM457, XM470–471, XM475–476, XN460, XN462, XN495, XN502–503, XN509, XN557, XN586, XN592–595, XN597; *T.4*, XP550, XP569, XP614, XP617, XP619–620, XP622–625, XP628–631, XP641–642, XP662, XP664–665, XP669, XP672–673, XP677, XP685, XR644, XR647–648, XR667, XR670–671, XR673, XR706, XS176–177, XS182–183.

Following preparation for RAF service by No. 27 MU at Shawbury, Jet Provost T.3 XM370 joined No. 2 FTS on 16 October 1959. (Hunting Group via R. L. Ward Collection)

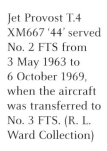

Jet Provost T.4 XM667 '44' served No. 2 FTS from 3 May 1963 to 6 October 1969, when the aircraft was transferred to No. 3 FTS. (R. L. Ward Collection)

No. 2 FTS's display team was originally called 'Viper Red' but during the 1968 and 1969 season was renamed 'The Vipers'. This is Jet Provost T.4 XR670, one of 'The Vipers'. (R. L. Ward Collection)

No. 3 Flying Training School   *Achieve*

A/c   T.3, 4 and 5
Dates   September 1961 to April 1984 and February 1989 to October 1991
Stations   Leeming, Cranwell
A/c: *T.3*, XM351–352, XM357–358, XM362, XM365, XM367–368, XM370–371, XM374–376, XM379, XM387, XM401, XM403–404, XM412, XM415–416, XM418–419, XM424–426, XM428, XM453, XM455, XM458–459, XM461, XM464, XM470–473, XN137; *T.4*, XP552, XP562, XP564, XP574, XP576–582, XP587, XP617–618, XP621, XP627, XP636, XP640, XP663, XP667, XP674, XP676, XP679, XP686–687, XR646, XR650–651, XR654, XR659, XR661, XR667, XR670, XR672, XR674–677, XR697–698, XR700, XR702–703, XS176–177, XS181–182, XS184–185, XS218, XS220, XS229; *T.5*, XW287, XW289–292, XW294–296, XW298, XW302, XW304–307, XW310–311, XW313–336, XW351–355, XW357, XW360–370, XW373–375, XW406–408, XW410–416, XW418, XW420–438.

Above: The process of becoming an RAF Phantom pilot (the aircraft in the background) was made much easier thanks to the Jet Provost. This is No. 3 FTS T.3 XN607 '4' at the SBAC in September 1968. (R. L. Ward)

Below: The gold lettering of the 'The Swords' can be just made out on the intake of Jet Provost T.5 XW428 '54'. The aircraft is taxiing at Greenham Common on 6 July 1974. (R. L. Ward)

No. 6 Flying Training School   *Aspice et Imitare (Look and Imitate)*

A/c   T.3, 4 and 5
Dates   August 1961 to June 1968 and May 1970 to August 1993
Stations   Acklington, Finningley

A/c: *T.3*, XM346, XM359, XM379, XM383, XM402, XM407, XM414, XM416–420, XM422, XM424, XM126, XM467–468, XM470–471, XM474, XM480, XN464, XN492, XN503, XN506, XN509, XN551, XN556, XN578, XN581, XN590, XN592, XN594, XN596, XN599–606, XN634, XN638–640; *T.4*, XP548, XP556–557, XP560, XP563–564, XP567, XP570–571, XP583, XP585, XP627, XP629, XP634–636, XP638, XP640, XP661–662, XP674, XP676, XP680, XP683, XP686, XR643–644, XR646–647, XR649, XR652, XR654, XR656, XR658–660, XR662–664, XR666–667, XR672–673, XR675, XR680–681, XR704, XR706; *T.5*, XW287, XW291, XW293, XW296, XW298, XW302, XW304, XW306–307, XW309, XW311, XW316, XW322, XW324–325, XW327, XW352, XW359, XW363, XW368, XW372, XW375, XW405, XW425, XW428–431, XW428.

Jet Provost T.4 XP657 'R' of No. 6 FTS climbs out of Greenham Common on 6 July 1974. (R. L. Ward)

No. 6 FTS Jet Provost T.5 XW309 'V' captured at RAF Finningley on 27 July 1977. (R. L. Ward)

No. 7 Flying Training School

A/c   T.3 and 4
Dates   March 1962 to September 1991
Station   Church Fenton

A/c: *T.3*, XM350–352, XM355–356, XM358–359, XM361, XM366, XM370, XM374, XM376, XM378, XM383, XM410, XM413–414, XM416–417, XM419, XM421, XM425, XM457, XM459, XM465–466, XM471–473, XM475–476, XM478, XN461–462, XN466, XN470, XN472–473, XN493, XN495, XN500, XN506, XN508–510, XN548, XN551–552, XN557, XN559, XN574–575, XN577, XN579, XN581–583, XN586, XN591, XN593–595, XN606, XN629–630, XN634, XN640; *T.4*, XP617, XP666, XP668, XP670, XP675, XP678–679, XP681–682, XP684–685, XR645–646, XR650–651, XR653, XR655, XR657–658, XR661–662, XR670, XR676, XS175, XS178; *T.5*, XW301, XW303, XW316, XW319, XW321, XW326–328, XW330, XW334, XW358–361, XW365, XW371–372, XW405, XW407, XW409, XW411, XW413, XW415–419, XW427, XW432–434.

No. 7 FTS Jet Provost T.4s XR653 'N' and XS175 'X', low and slow over RAF Odiham on 10 September 1964. (R. L. Ward)

Jet Provost T.5A XW360 '129/CF' of No. 7 FTS at RAF Abingdon on 12 September 1981. (R. L. Ward)

Royal Air Force College   *Superna Petimus* (*We seek higher things*)

A/c   T.3, 4 & 5
Dates   June 1960 to December 1991
Stations   Cranwell

A/c: *T.3*, XM346, XM349–350, XM358, XM361, XM366, XM371, XM374–376, XM383, XM405, XM410, XM414, XM419, XM424–425, XM427, XM451–456, XM458–467, XM469, XM471, XM475, XM479, XN468, XN471–473, XN492–500, XN505–506, XN509–510, XN547–548, XN551–553, XN555, XN558–559, XN577–590, XN605, XN629–630, XN634–636, XN640–641; *T.4*, XP547–548, XP555–570, XP575, XP583–XP586, XP624, XP667–668, XP671, XP673, XP688, XR643, XR654, XR656, XR662, XR673, XR675, XR679, XR681, XR707, XS177–179, XS181–182, XS185, XS217, XS222; *T.5*, XW287–292, XW295–296, XW299, XW302, XW305, XW307, XW310, XW313–318, XW320–323, XW325, XW327–328, XW330, XW332–336, XW351–369, XW372–374, XW405–406, XW408, XW410–413, XW416–417, XW419–423, XW425 & XW436–438

Above: Jet Provost T.4 XP564 '79' of the RAF College climbs out of RAF Cranwell *c.* 1965. The aircraft was lost on 22 April 1982 while serving with the TWU. (R. L. Ward Collection)

Below: On board with the RAFC 'The Poachers' tight over Cranwell in 1976, their final year as a display team. (MoD/Crown Copyright (TN 7500/3) via R. L. Ward Collection)

College of Air Warfare

A/c   T.4
Dates   1962 to 1974
Stations   Manby
A/c; **T.4**, XP549, XP551, XP558, XP575, XP580, XP583, XP625, XP629, XP632, XP638, XP640, XP672, XP680, XP686, XR646, XR649 651, XR653 654, XR658, XR660, XR662, XR667, XR670, XR672, XR674, XR679, XR701, XR704–705, XS176–177, XS179–180, XS186, XS209–216, XS218–219 & XS226

Jet Provost T.4 XP686 '32', one of 'The Macaws' for the 1968 season, performing at Biggin Hill on 11 May. (R. L. Ward)

School of Refresher Flying/Refresher Flying Squadron

A/c   T.4
Dates   1962 to 1984
Stations Manby, Leeming, Church Fenton
A/c, *T.4*, XP547, XP556, XP563, XP629, XP672, XP688, XR650–651, XR653, XR662, XR670, XR672–674, XR701, XS176–177, XS211, XS215 & XS217–219

Jet Provost XS215 '18' pictured at RAF Manby. This aircraft served the CAW and SoRF. (R. L. Ward Collection)

Central Air Traffic Control School

A/c   T.3 & 4
Dates   c. 1975 to Jul 1989
Station   Shawbury
A/c: *T.3*, XM376; *T.4*, XP547, XP556, XP563–564, XP567, XP629, XP638, XP640, XP672, XP686, XP688, XR650–651, XR653, XR660, XR662, XR667, XR670, XR672–4, XR679, XR681, XR700–701, XS176–178, XS181, XS211, XS215, XS217 & XS219

TWU (Tactical Weapons Unit) & No. 1 TWU

A/c   T.3 & 4
Dates   September 1974 to July 1978 (TWU) and July 1978 to 1990
Station   Shawbury
A/c (TWU): *T.3*, XM475 (also served as 'F' with 229 OCU), XN471, XN579, XN584; *T.4*, XS177. A/c (1 TWU): *T.4*, XP547, XP564, XP638, XR679, XR701, XS178, XS181 & XS219

Transferred from the CATCS in March 1982, Jet Provost T.4 XS219 '06' served out her RAF flying days with No. 1 TWU until 1989. (R. L. Ward Collection)

No. 3 CAACU

A/c: *T.4*, XP558, XR643, XR679

No. 27 MU

A/c: *T.4*, XR701, XS218

Jet Provost T.3 XM460 pictured at No. 27 MU, RAF Shawbury, on 17 July 1960 before delivery to its first unit, the RAFC, on 19 July. (R. L. Ward)

No. 27 MU was responsible for preparing the majority of the RAF's Jet Provost fleet and, towards the end of their careers, their disposal. Jet Provost T.3 XM463 is also pictured on 17 July 1960; she was destined to be delivered to the RAFC a few days later. (R. L. Ward)

No. 26 Squadron

A/c   T.3
Dates   July 1974 to October 1977
Stations   Wyton, Cranwell
A/c: *T.3*, XM453, XM455, XM459, XM475, XN500, XN506, XN643

A&AEE

A/c: *T.1*, XD674-676; *T.2*, XD694; *T.3*, XM346–350, XM352, XM383, XN117 (ex-T.2 G-23-1), XN463, XN467, XN503; *T.4*, XP547, XR701

Armstrong Siddeley

A/c: *T.1*, XD674

BFTS Cranwell

A/c: *T.5*, XW298

Bristol Siddeley Engines

A/c: *T.3*, XM353, XM383, XM458, XN463, XN468; *T.4*, XP573

CFE

A/c: *T.3*, XM421

Controller (Aircraft)

A/c: *T.3*, XM347

Handling Squadron

A/c: *T.1*, XD677; *T.2*, XD694; *T.4*, XP548, XP639

Hunting-Percival/Hunting

A/c: *T.1*, XD674, XD678; *T.3*, XM346, XM348, XM365, XM456, XN467

Jet Provost Trials Unit

A/c: *T.4*, XS221, XS223–224

MinTech

A/c: *T.3*, XM474, XN503

MoA

A/c: *T.3*, XM474, XN591, XR669

MoD(PE)

A/c. T.3, XN459, XN629; *T.4*, XP547, XP558, XR701; *T.5*, XW298, XW306, XW317, XW425

Ministry of Supply

A/c: *T.3*, XM346

Station Flight, St Athan

A/c: *T.3*, XN553

In Civilian Hands

Because of their relative economy compared to the average military jet, plus an abundance of spares, a large number of Jet Provost and Strikemaster aircraft were kept airworthy (and many still are) in civilian hands. The Jet Provost/Strikemaster family have become regular additions to air shows across the globe since their retirement from the RAF during the early 1990s. Here are just a few examples from recent years.

Jet Provost T.3 (later T.3A) XM370 entered service with No. 2 FTS on 16 October 1959 and was one of several aircraft purchased by Global Aviation at Binbrook in late 1993. Registered as G-BVSP, the aircraft is pictured at Fairford/RIAT on 19 July 2004 under the ownership of H. G. Hodges & Sons Ltd. (R. L. Ward)

Above: XM378 first entered service with No. 2 FTS on 21 December 1959 and bowed out with No. 1 FTS in 1993. The T.3A joined the civilian register as G-BWZE and is pictured at RAF Coltishall on 2 October 1998. (R. L. Ward)

Below: XM478's long RAF career began with No. 1 FTS on 28 September 1960, the aircraft ending is service days at No. 1 SoTT at RAF Halton. With the civilian registration G-BXDL, the aircraft is pictured on the static line at RIAT on 19 July 2002. (R. L. Ward)

Above: T.3A XM479 (G-BVES) was operated by the Newcastle Jet Provost Group when the aircraft was captured at RIAT on 19 July 2004. (R. L. Ward)

Below: The Jet Provost Club T.4, XR679 (G-BWGT), on the static line at RNAS Yeovilton on 13 July 1996. (R. L. Ward)

Above: Jet Provost T.4 XR679 (G-BWGT) with a new scheme at RAF Waddington on 30 June 2004. (R. L. Ward)

Below: The prototype T.5 (T.5P), XS230, is another survivor which was sold via an MoD auction in 1994. Registered as G-VIVM, the pristine aircraft is pictured at Fairford on 20 July 1996. (R. L. Ward)

Above: Still wearing its CFS badge on the forward fuselage from its last RAF unit is T.5A XW433, re-registered as G-JPRO. The aircraft, in company with an airworthy piston Provost, is at RIAT, RAF Cottesmore, on 30 July 2001. (R. L. Ward)

Below: Ex-RSAF Strikemaster Mk 80 1112 makes for an impressive sight with this colour scheme. Registered as G-FLYY, the aircraft is pictured at RAF Waddington on 30 June 2004. (R. L. Ward)

Above: This Strikemaster Mk 87 first entered service with the Kenyan Air Force in 1970 and finished its military career with the Botswana Defence Force. Registered as G-UNNY, the aircraft is displaying its BDF serial OJ4 on the nose. The aircraft is pictured at RNAS Yeovilton on 18 July 1998. (R. L. Ward)

Below: Another ex-BDF Strikemaster Mk 87, registered as G-UVNR, at RAF Waddington on 30 June 2004. (R. L. Ward)

Despite being presented in RNZAF markings with a genuine serial, this is actually another ex-BDF Strikemaster Mk 87, 'OJ5'. The aircraft is on the flight line at RNAS Yeovilton on 18 July 1998. (R. L. Ward)

Glossary

A&AEE	Aeroplane & Armament Experimental Establishment
AFC	Air Force Cross
ASV	Armstrong Siddeley Viper
AUW	All-Up Weight
BAC	British Aircraft Corporation
BDF	Botswana Defence Force
BFTS	Basic Flying Training School
CAC	Commonwealth Aircraft Corporation
CATCS	Central Air Traffic Control School
CAW	College of Air Warfare
CFE	Central Fighter Establishment
CFS	Central Flying School
COIN	COunter INsurgency
DB	Disbanded
DBR	Damaged Beyond Repair
DF	Direction Finding
DME	Distance Measuring Equipment
EFTS	Elementary Flying Training School
FAA	Fleet Air Arm
Flt Lt	Flight Lieutenant
FRAeS	Fellowship of the Royal Aeronautical Society
FTS	Flying Training School
GAF	Australian General Aircraft Factory
MoD	Ministry of Defence
MoS	Ministry of Supply
MU	Maintenance Unit
OCU	Operation Conversion Unit
OR	Operational Requirement
PAF	Portuguese Air Force
QFI	Qualified Flying Instructor
QRA	Quick Reaction Alert
RAAF	Royal Australian Air Force
RAE	Royal Aircraft Establishment
RAF	Royal Air Force
RAFC	Royal Air Force College
RAFVR	Royal Air Force Volunteer Reserve
RF	Reformed

RIAT	Royal International Air Tattoo
RN	Royal Navy
RNAS	Royal Naval Air Station
RNZAF	Royal New Zealand Air Force
RP	Rocket Projectile
SFOM	Société Francaise d'Optique et de Mechanique
SNEB	Societé Nouvelle des Establissements Edgar Brandt
SOC	Struck off Charge
SoRF	School of Refresher Flying
SoTT	School of Technical Training
VHF	Very High Frequency
VOR	Omni-Directional Range
WFU	Withdrawn from Use

Bibliography

Collier Webb, Derek, *UK Flight Testing Accidents 1940–71* (Air Britain).

Haig-Thomas, Tony, *Fall Out Roman Catholics and Jews* (Old Forge Publishing).

Halley, James J., *RAF Aircraft XA100–XZ999* (Air Britain).

Silvester, John, *Percival & Hunting Aircraft* (Nelson and Saunders).

Sturtivant, Ray and John Hamlin, *Flying Training and Support Aircraft Since 1912* (Air Britain).

Thetford, Owen, *Aircraft of the Royal Air Force Since 1918* (Putnam).

Watkins, David, *From Jet Provost to Strikemaster* (Grub Street).